I0162082

Looking For Love

Raymond Hopkins

SILVERMOON
PUBLISHING
www.silvermonpublishing.co.uk

SILVERMOON

P U B L I S H I N G

A Division of Silvermoon Productions Limited
3rd Floor | 207 Regent Street | London | W1B 3HH
0207 096 0979
www.silvermoonpublishing.co.uk

ISBN 978-1-910457-16-0

Silvermoon Publishing is an innovative publishing house established to publish plays and license rights to theatre companies world-wide. Silvermoon aims to promote its plays and playwrights to ensure that its playwrights get maximum exposure.

Recordings of the songs mentioned in the text are not covered by licences issued by Silvermoon Publishing. The use of these recordings should be declared to the PERFORMING RIGHTS SOCIETY in the usual manner.

VIDEO-RECORDING OF AMATEUR PRODUCTIONS

Please note that the copyright laws governing video-recording are extremely complex and that it should not be assumed that any play may be video-recorded for whatever purpose without first obtaining the permission of the appropriate agents. The fact that a play is published by Silvermoon Publishing does not indicate that video rights are available or that Silvermoon Publishing control such rights.

PERFORMING LICENCE APPLICATIONS

A performing licence for these plays will be issued by "Silvermoon Publishing" subject to the following conditions:-

1. That the performance fee is paid in full on the date of application for a licence.
2. That the name of the author(s) is/are clearly shown in any programme or publicity material.
3. That the author(s) is/are entitled to receive two complimentary tickets to see his/her/their work in performance if they so wish.
4. That a copy of the play is purchased from Silvermoon Publishing for each named speaking part and a minimum of three copies purchased for backstage use.
5. That a copy of any reviews / Marketing materials be forwarded to Silvermoon Publishing.
6. That the Silvermoon Publishing licensing statement be displayed on any marketing material.

FEES

Details of script prices and fees payable for each performance or public reading can be obtained by telephone to (+44) 0207 096 0979 or to the address below. Alternatively, latest prices can be obtained from our website. www.silvermoonpublishing.co.uk.

To apply for a performing licence for any play please write to Silvermoon Publishing, 3rd Floor, 207 Regent Street, London W1B 3HH or email via our website with the following details:-

1.   Name and address of theatre company.
2.   Details of venue including seating capacity.
3.   Dates of proposed performance or public reading.
4.   Contact telephone number for Author's complimentary tickets.

Or apply directly via our website at www.silvermoonpublishing.co.uk

PROFESSIONAL RIGHTS

Professional rights for Looking For Love should be addressed to Silvermoon Publishing.

The author of LOOKING FOR LOVE, Raymond Hopkins, is donating his share of the proceeds to MULTIPLE SCLEROSIS RESEARCH.

LOOKING FOR LOVE

Synopsis

After twenty-one years of marriage, James Beale walks out on his wife, Molly. She is devastated and after four months of being alone, she has reached rock bottom. Her best friend, Fiona, persuades her to try the "six-step miracle cure" for abandoned wives. The idea being, on completion, she will be guaranteed to get her life back together.

Molly agrees and finds that it works. Not only does her husband want to come back, but she has two other suitors vying for her affection. The twists and turns, the intrigues, the misunderstandings on her road to recovery, all add up to a hilarious evening's entertainment.

ACT ONE

Scene I	Monday morning
Scene II	Tuesday afternoon (two weeks later)
Scene III	The following Friday evening

ACT TWO

Scene I	The following Monday morning
Scene II	Thursday, late afternoon
Scene III	Friday, late morning

The Beales live in a small town in the Midlands. The action of the play takes place in the lounge of their semi-detached house. It is late spring – the present day.

CAST IN ORDER OF APPEARANCE

MOLLY BEALE - Wife of James. About forty-five. Since her husband left her, she lacks confidence and finds life hard going. After the first scene, looks very good for her age. By the end of the play she is transformed and has become a new woman!

FIONA BROADBENT - Lifelong best friend of Molly. About forty-four. Does not take life too seriously. Lots of energy. Dresses in quirky clothes. Has had lots of men friends. Full of charisma.

CLAIRE PEARSON - Daughter of James and Molly. About twenty-one. Smart in appearance. Married with one child. Feels torn between her parents since the breakdown of their marriage.

NANCY GROVES - Neighbour. About sixty-eight. Shabbily dressed and poorly groomed in Act One. Slight improvement in Act Two. A real bore. She is besotted with her dog since her husband died.

LYN HARRIS - Friend from church. About thirty. Fairly plain in appearance. Conservatively dressed and well-groomed. She is single and has high moral principles. Well-educated. Saving herself for the Rev. David Thomas.

JAMES BEALE - Husband of Molly. About forty-nine. Good-looking and smart in appearance. Well-educated and has good social skills. He comes across as a very likeable person. He is a romantic at heart.

PAUL TRITTON - Friend from church. About seventy-two. Not much dress sense. Lives alone since his wife died. Does not always think before he speaks. Churchgoer but is also worldly-wise.

THE REV. DAVID THOMAS - About thirty-five. Not married. Smart in appearance. Well-educated. A very saintly Christian who has dedicated his life to the church. He is shy and naive when it comes to females. His romantic passions have never been switched on! Recently moved into the parish.

STEVE MILES - About thirty-one. Smart, good-looking and oozing with virility. Well-built and super fit. Girls love him! Works at a health spa, as a masseur.

ACT I

Scene I

When the curtain rises, the stage is empty and the telephone is ringing. Molly enters from the kitchen and answers the phone. She looks tired and dowdy. She hasn't got any make-up on. Her hair is a mess.

MOLLY
(*Subdued voice*) Hello … (*Getting cross*) I told you never to bother me again … How am I? Wonderful, thank you. In fact, these last four months have been the best I've ever had … (*Shouting*) You what? You walked out after twenty-one years of marriage to set up a love nest with a blonde bimbo. Why would I want to be your friend? … Actually you've done me a favour. (*Ecstatically*) I've never been so happy in my entire life. Don't ring again. I'll be out on the town, enjoying myself. (*Slams down receiver and bursts into tears. After a few seconds the phone rings – Molly stops crying and picks up receiver*) What do you want now, you perverted pig? … Oh, hello, Vicar … Yes, I'm coping extremely well with the break-up, thank you … Choir practice next week … All right, I'll try and make it … Nice of you to ring … Bye. (*Replaces receiver. Turns radio on – it is playing 'I miss you like crazy' by Natalie Cole. Molly turns off radio and bursts into tears again. Doorbell rings. Molly stops crying and exits to hall*)

FIONA
(*Off*)   Just popped round to see how things are.

MOLLY
(*Entering with Fiona*) Well, let's just say over these past four months, my life's been flushed down the loo.

FIONA
(*Hugging Molly*) Things are never as bad as they seem.

MOLLY
(*Moving away*) Are you joking? Since that rotten maggot walked out, my whole world's been falling apart. (*Pause*) On our wedding day, in front of a hundred witnesses, he said, "to love and to cherish till death us do part," and I naively assumed he was telling me the truth.

FIONA
There's a very easy way to tell when a man's lying. Just watch their lips: every time they move, that's when they'll be lying.

MOLLY	I don't know what I'd have done without your support. How long have we been best friends?
FIONA	Since our school days.
MOLLY	That seems like a lifetime ago.
FIONA	(*Philosophically*) That's because it is a lifetime ago. (*Pause*) Right, the first thing you've got to do is stop blaming yourself.
MOLLY	(*Looking shocked*) Well, actually, I wasn't blaming myself. I've never given that Casanova any reason to leave me. I've washed, cooked and cleaned for him. I mopped his brow when he was suffering from man flu. I comforted him when he got stressed at work. I never made a fuss when he left the loo seat up.
FIONA	What were things like between the sheets?
MOLLY	I moaned and groaned in all the right places. I told him he made love like a stallion, although in recent years he's been more like a carthorse. What is it about men? Why are they never satisfied with what they've got?
FIONA	They can't help themselves. All it takes is a flirtatious glance from a pretty female and their brain goes into overdrive. Animal instincts take over, and they go into self-destruct mode. (*Sarcastically*) You've almost got to feel sorry for the poor darlings.
MOLLY	Are you serious?
FIONA	By the time they've checked out the promised land, and their libido levels have returned to normal, it's too late. (*Philosophically*) They've ruined everyone's lives.
MOLLY	(*Getting cross*) When I got married, I had an hourglass figure, and a blemish-free skin. (*Looking in the wall mirror*) Now look at me. My face is wrinkled and pitted. My waist and hips are fighting the battle of the bulge. My bra's given up trying to support my sagging bosom. My teeth have got more fillings than a toasted sandwich. (*In desperation*) What chance have I got of finding another partner?

FIONA	Now you've put it like that, I suppose things are looking pretty bleak.
MOLLY	I've given that man the best years of my life.
FIONA	(*Looking at Molly*) No-one can argue with that.
MOLLY	(*With despair*) I'll never be seeing my fortieth birthday again.
FIONA	What's more, your fiftieth's looming on the horizon.
MOLLY	(*Getting cross*) Will you please stop agreeing with me?
FIONA	You should have been like me. I've never given myself to any one man. Before they have chance to tire of me, I move on.
MOLLY	How many partners have you got through?
FIONA	I'm on number six at the moment. Once they mention wedding bells, I hear alarm bells.
MOLLY	(*Sorrowfully*) Everything I'd hoped and dreamed for has disappeared overnight.
FIONA	Don't let worrying about tomorrow spoil today. You've got to stop wasting your life, enjoy every minute of it. There are a lot of people worse off than you.
MOLLY	Don't you think I know that. (*Pause*) I want to hate him but I can't. Yesterday I was looking through our wedding photos. (*Reflectively*) Those first few years were magical: we were soulmates.
FIONA	(*Assertively*) It's time for you to face facts. There's no lifetime guarantee with a marriage.
MOLLY	What are all the church members going to say?
FIONA	Well, it'll make a change from them gossiping about the choirmaster's fling with the mayor's wife.
MOLLY	All my emotions are shot to bits. I've never felt so alone. (*Crying*) I don't know what I'm going to do.

FIONA	Accept the fact your life's never going to be the same. Then you've got two choices. Your first one is to …
MOLLY	I'm certainly not having him back.
FIONA	Actually, I don't think that's going to happen. (*Awkwardly*) I caught a glimpse of his new lady friend yesterday. Once he's sampled the truly irresistible range, he's unlikely to come back to something that's past its sell-by date.
MOLLY	(*Stops crying – getting cross*) Hang on a minute, what are you implying?
FIONA	I'm being realistic. I'd say your first choice is to go on the happy pills.
MOLLY	I don't fancy becoming a pill-popper.
FIONA	Don't knock it, dear. There are an awful lot of women who rely on their daily dose of diazepam.
MOLLY	So what's my second choice?
FIONA	Give the Marital merry-go-round a spin.
MOLLY	(*Completely mystified*) What are you on about?
FIONA	That's the title of a book which was written by a woman whose husband left her on the day of their Silver wedding anniversary. It was a best-seller. (*Getting book from handbag*) I bought a copy a while ago.
MOLLY	(*Looking vague*) Marital merry-go-round?
FIONA	It's been hailed as a miracle cure for women who've been jilted. The book lists some radical steps that'll get you on the road to recovery. You work your way through six objectives, and on completion, you're guaranteed to get your life back on track. I've not mentioned the book to you before, but I think you've reached the last resort stage. These are desperate times.
MOLLY	So you're saying it'll restore my self-confidence and lift me out of the depressive state I'm in?

FIONA	(*Looking through book*) I've got a couple of friends who've tried it and never looked back. I'd recommend it to any woman who's been left in the lurch. One woman who went on it was remarried within a couple of weeks of her divorce.
MOLLY	I'm going for it. I've got nothing to lose.
FIONA	The only stipulation is that you mustn't tell anyone you're doing it.
MOLLY	Sounds intriguing. (*Pause*) So when do I start?
FIONA	(*Looking through book*) There's no time like the present. Just remember, you must complete every task to reach your goal. It's only then you'll regain your self-esteem and be firmly back in control of your own destiny.
MOLLY	Okay, so what's the first thing I've got to do?
FIONA	(*Reading from book*) Visit a spa.
MOLLY	(*Looking confused*) I can go to the Spar corner shop any day of the week. How will that help me?
FIONA	You've certainly lost contact with the finer things of life. I'm on about a health spa.
MOLLY	How ever much will that cost?
FIONA	(*Looking closely at Molly*) At least six hundred quid. You're going to need the full works. (*Reading from book*) The author's called the first chapter 'Flaunting your assets'. This is where the therapy begins. (*To Molly*) What do you see when you get out of bed and look in the mirror?
MOLLY	Not a lot, my eyes are fading fast.
FIONA	(*Putting book back into handbag*) That's probably just as well. Look, let's be perfectly honest with each other. You're a dowdy middle aged woman, with about as much sex appeal as a dead slug. (*Molly looks horrified*) After the health spa you'll need to buy yourself some fashionable gear.

MOLLY	I don't think I can afford to do it.
FIONA	I don't think you can afford not to do it. Surely you've got some spare cash stashed away for a rainy day, because from where I'm standing, a monsoon's heading in your direction.
MOLLY	I'll go to the bank right now and draw out every penny I can get from our joint account. I'll show that loser.
FIONA	Now you're talking. I'll pop home and sort out a good spa. In fact, I've already got one in mind; it's called 'Sunrise Health Spa'. (*Pause*) This is the start of your new beginning. (*With confidence*) We're going to turn your life around. (*Hugging Molly*) Bye. (*Exits to hall*)

(*Molly exits to kitchen and returns with a coat, which she puts on a chair. She goes over to a wall mirror and studies herself. Claire enters from hall*)

CLAIRE	Hi, Mum. What's the latest news?
MOLLY	(*Getting cross*) The latest news is that your dad's phoned (*sarcastically*) and wants to be my friend.
CLAIRE	(*Enthusiastically*) Oh, that's nice.
MOLLY	(*Getting cross*) YOU WHAT? You don't think I'm having anything more to do with him, do you?
CLAIRE	I can't see why not.
MOLLY	In case it's escaped your attention, that man's ruined my life. (*Rubbing the bags under her eyes*) I've not slept for the past four months.
CLAIRE	Join the club. Since I gave birth to Tom, I've not slept at all. (*Sarcastically*) Whereas my dear husband manages to sleep whatever.
MOLLY	(*Getting cross*) There is a subtle difference. You savoured the fruits of nature, resulting in the birth of your twenty-one month old son. Whereas your dad savoured the fruits of nature, resulting in the death of our twenty-one year marriage.

CLAIRE	I really think you and Dad should get together and talk about the future.
MOLLY	Your dad and I haven't got a future. Still, it's nice to know you're concerned about my wellbeing.
CLAIRE	Actually, I was more concerned about my inheritance. (*Looking worried*) If he remarries, I could miss out big time.
MOLLY	I can't believe I'm hearing this.
CLAIRE	In any case, it's not all Dad's fault. There are always two sides to every story.
MOLLY	(*Getting cross*) Yes, and you've always taken your dad's side. (*Phone rings*) You get it; I can't face anyone at the moment.
CLAIRE	(*Answering phone*) Hello … Oh, hello, Dad … Yes, I'm fine thanks, how about you? … (*Sympathetically*) Are you being looked after? … (*Molly tuts disapprovingly*) Oh, right … (*Speaking to Molly*) Mum, Dad wants a word with you.
MOLLY	I've already told that low-life to wrap up.
CLAIRE	(*Speaking into phone*) She says she can't come to the phone at the moment, but hopes you're keeping warm.
MOLLY	(*Shouting at the phone*) Tell him he's left his Viagra tablets here, so when his new lady friend's baking, she'll need to double up on the self-raising flour. (*Picking up coat*) I'm going out for a while. Lock the door on your way out. (*Exits to kitchen*)
CLAIRE	(*Speaking into phone*) Oh, Dad, whatever made you go off like that? … You're acting like a teenager … Why didn't you join the bowls club like all the other men of your age? … Mum's in a right state … Well, it's a bit late to say that now … All right, I'll call round and have a chat … That woman's not going to be there, is she? … Right, I'll see you in a few minutes … (*Doorbell rings*) I've got to go, there's someone at the door … Love you, bye. (*Replaces receiver and exits to hall - Off*) Hello, Mrs Groves, I'm afraid Mum's not here, and I'm just on my way out.

NANCY	(*Entering from hall, followed by Claire*) I'm not stopping long. I just wanted an update on the latest news. I'm off to the church coffee morning and people are bound to ask what's happening.
CLAIRE	(*Getting cross*) Well, tell them that nothing's happening.
NANCY	I suppose he hit the mid-life crisis. Mrs Smyth was telling me it happened to her husband. He reached fifty, got himself a tattoo of a snake eating a rat. Had his ear pierced, bought himself one of them Harley Davidster motorbikes and disappeared into the sunset with the barmaid from the Spyglass and Kettle. (*Pause*) My Frank was never like that. He was a homemaker. (*With sadness*) Since he passed away, my life's not been the same. If it hadn't been for Willy, I don't know what I'd have done.
CLAIRE	(*Uninterestedly*) And how's your dog been keeping?
NANCY	He's been doing well, thank you. I call him my little baby, although he's sixteen next month. The only trouble is he's having a job controlling his bowels. He's been leaving me presents all over the house, the little rascal.
CLAIRE	(*Sarcastically*) He sounds like a real bundle of fun.
NANCY	Thinking about it, my little baby could be the answer to your mum's problems. Now your dad's cleared off, your mum'll need to get a job. She could do a bit of cleaning for me. (*Looking around the room*) My daughter's been looking for a semi. If your mum wants a quick sale without going through an estate agent, we could do a deal.
CLAIRE	I don't think Mum's got any intention of selling.
NANCY	(*Looking disgruntled*) Surely with your dad doing a runner, she'll need to sort out her finances.
CLAIRE	(*Getting impatient*) Yes, well, I really must be getting on.
NANCY	Tell your mum I'll pop in and see her soon.
CLAIRE	(*Unconvincingly*) She'll be pleased.

NANCY	That's what neighbours are for, dear. (*Looking at her watch*) Is that the time? I need to go, or that Mrs Jones'll be sitting in my place. She's got cod.
CLAIRE	I didn't realize they served meals at the coffee morning.
NANCY	They don't. I'm on about that C.O.D. You know, she can't stop washing her hands.
CLAIRE	I think you mean O.C.D. (*Aside*) That's one thing you'll never suffer with.
NANCY	I suppose you can't blame your dad for trying to better himself. I've heard his new lady friend's quite well-off. See you soon. Bye. (*Exits to hall*)

(*Claire walks over to the wall mirror and puts some lipstick on. The doorbell rings*)

CLAIRE	(*Walking to hall exit*) What's that stupid woman forgotten now? (*Exits to hall – Off*) Oh, hello, Lyn. Come in.
LYN	(*Entering with Claire*) Could I have a word with Molly?
CLAIRE	She's out. Can I help?
LYN	I've just been having a coffee with David, and he suggested that your mum …
CLAIRE	Sorry, David who?
LYN	The Reverend David Thomas. He's just been on the phone to your mum, and he forgot to ask her if she'd lead a discussion on the perils of alcohol. I believe she's been teetotal all her life.
CLAIRE	Yes, she signed the pledge at sixteen.
LYN	David's going to hold a public meeting, making people aware that we've got to improve our moral standards. He said that the fabric of our society's being torn apart. He's asked me to lead a discussion on chastity. (*With disdain*) Girls give up their innocence nowadays at the whim of some lustful man. Paul, the church organist, will be dealing with the evils of drugs, and we're hoping

your mum will speak on abstinence from alcohol. David's suggested we get together at the church two weeks Friday at 7.30 to plan out our strategy. Would your mum be up to joining us?

CLAIRE   I'm sure she would. It'll give her something else to think about. (*Pause*) I'll tell you what; why not hold your get together here? That'll be much better for Mum.

LYN   Oh right, I'll put David in the picture.

CLAIRE   I'll tell Mum . So that's 7.30 two weeks on Friday?

LYN   That's right. (*With affection*) David's such a wonderful man. He's only been here six months and he's put so much work into our community. Only last week he ran a soup kitchen for the down-and-outs. The only problem was, some of the local high-spirited teenagers had laced the soup with a couple of bottles of vodka. We couldn't understand why everybody was coming back for more. It was only when David had a cupful of soup and went into a drunken stupor that we figured out what they'd done.

CLAIRE   The vicar isn't married, is he?

LYN   (*With confidence*) Not yet, but I'm working on it. (*Pause*) I'm so sorry to hear about your dad leaving.

CLAIRE   He's been a wonderful dad to me. I can't believe he'd be so stupid. I guess it's the male menopause.

LYN   (*Looking at her watch*) I really must be going. I've promised to make David a few fairy cakes: they're his favourite.

CLAIRE   I'll come with you. I'm on my way to see Dad now. (*Claire and Lyn exit to hall – The phone rings and goes onto answerphone*)

JAMES   (*Speaking on answerphone*) It's me. I know you told me not to keep ringing, but I've got to talk to you. Please give me a call.

Blackout

Scene II

When the curtain rises, Fiona is sitting on the sofa.

FIONA   (*Shouting to kitchen*) What time's your mum due back?

CLAIRE   (*Off*) About two thirty. (*Pause*) I still don't understand what made her go to a health spa, and why I was sworn to secrecy? I wasn't even allowed to tell, Dad.

FIONA   (*Unconvincingly*) I've no idea. In any case why should people want to know her business?

CLAIRE   (*Off*) It just seems rather strange. (*Pause*) How many sugars?

FIONA   (*Shouting to kitchen exit*) I shouldn't really, but I'll have three please. (*Looking thoughtful*) Why does partaking of the pleasurable things in life always make me feel guilty?

(*Claire enters from kitchen carrying two cups of tea. She hands one to Fiona*)

      Thanks. (*Pause*) Every time I eat a bar of chocolate, I feel pangs of remorse. If I get stuck into a cream cake, I need counselling to ease my conscience.

CLAIRE   It's probably something to do with Adam and Eve in the garden of Eden. (*Clarifying*) Tasting the forbidden fruit.

FIONA   Of course. That's when they first realized they'd got some naughty bits, and covered them with fig leaves.

CLAIRE   So I guess ever since then anything pleasurable causes feelings of guilt.

FIONA   That's why people used to get married. It stopped them feeling guilty about making love.

CLAIRE   (*Looking thoughtful*) When I was young I wanted to marry someone just like my dad. He couldn't do any wrong in my eyes, and now look at him.

FIONA   That's why I've never married. It can be a battlefield with no winners. My dad always used to say to me: "When it comes to marriage, for the first six months you could eat your wife, and for the rest of your life you wish you had."

CLAIRE	How can two people who've had so much love for each other turn it into hate?
FIONA	If someone could come up with an answer to that, all the divorce lawyers would be forced to sell their posh houses and flashy cars.
MOLLY	(*Entering from hall – New hairstyle, chic outfit, full makeover: she looks stunning*) Hi, I'm back. (*Fiona and Claire both stare at Molly in amazement*) Well, say something.
FIONA	(*Getting off sofa and walking over to Molly*) You look absolutely stunning.
CLAIRE	(*Walking over to Molly*) I've never seen you look so gorgeous, Mum.
MOLLY	Thank you. I must admit I feel great. I've never been pampered so much in my entire life.
FIONA	You're like a different person. (*Seriously*) You're actually beautiful.
MOLLY	(*Looking bewildered*) I suppose I should take that as a compliment.
CLAIRE	So, tell us all about it.
MOLLY	The 'Sunrise Health Spa' has been an amazing experience. I loved the gymnasium, the pool, the jacuzzi, the hair and beauty salon, having a manicure. (*Pause*) Actually, if I had to pick one thing, it would be the massage parlour.
FIONA	That must have been totally relaxing.
MOLLY	Are you joking? By the time it was over, I was completely worn out. Each day I had this fit, virile young man with bulging biceps and the firmest six-pack you've ever seen giving me his undivided attention for an hour.
FIONA	So, why would you find that tiring?
MOLLY	You try holding your stomach in and lifting your sagging boobs for that long. It nearly killed me.

CLAIRE	What about the food?
MOLLY	It was succulent, but without the calories.
FIONA	That's a contradiction in terms.
MOLLY	Every morning I'd draw back the curtains to open countryside, having been woken up by the dawn chorus.
FIONA	My partner's flatulence always wakes me up.
CLAIRE	(*Getting out her mobile*) I'm ringing Dad. I want him to get a look at you and realize what he's given up.
MOLLY	Don't you dare.
CLAIRE	(*Dialling number on her mobile phone*) Why not? It might bring him to his senses. I'll be back in a couple of minutes. (*Walking to hall exit – speaking into phone*) Dad, it's me.
MOLLY	Come back here, this minute … (*Claire exits to hall*)
FIONA	Let her go. It'll do him good to find out what he's given up.
MOLLY	He left a message the other day asking me to ring him, but I'm not ready to do that yet.
FIONA	You soon will be. We're well on the way to turning your life around.
MOLLY	Well, I must say, the first step on the road to recovery's certainly been a great success. (*Looking in the wall mirror*) I've never felt so good about myself. (*Pause*) So what's my next step?
FIONA	Tell the truth.
MOLLY	(*Looking surprised*) What are you on about? (*Indignantly*) I always tell the truth.
FIONA	No, you don't. In fact, none of us do. For the next forty-eight hours you haven't got to lie to anyone, about anything. Tell people exactly what you're thinking, whether they want to hear it or not.

MOLLY	So you're saying I'm to speak my mind, irrespective of the consequences.
FIONA	That's right. I read the book from cover to cover last night. It makes compulsive reading. The author states that half the problems in a marriage are caused by couples not being totally honest with each other.
MOLLY	Surely that's called having tact?
FIONA	Call it what you want. For the next two days you're going to express your innermost thoughts.
MOLLY	I'm not in the habit of upsetting people.
FIONA	Look, you've told me you're feeling good about yourself. Now you need to gain the confidence to assert yourself without fear of retribution.
MOLLY	Oh, all right, I'll do it.
FIONA	So let's start with someone who's not going to take offence. I know you'll have a job to find any faults with me, but have a go.
MOLLY	(*Looking thoughtful*) You're a control freak.
FIONA	(*Looking surprised*) A control freak?
MOLLY	Yes, and you have a tendency to put yourself first. (*With confidence*) What's more, you can be quite moody at times. (*Pause*) You're not offended, are you?
FIONA	(*Unconvincingly*) Not at all. (*Getting cross*) It's not every day I get to hear that I'm a self-centred, control freak, who's prone to being a moody cow.
MOLLY	You told me to be honest. What's more, I think you're a fantastic mate. (*Molly hugs Fiona*) I wouldn't change you for the world.
FIONA	I can see you're going to find this challenge very interesting.
MOLLY	I probably won't have any friends at the end of it.

FIONA	(*Getting book from handbag and reading it*) By the way, I'll need to prepare you for your next objective.
MOLLY	But I thought I could only deal with one at a time.
FIONA	That's true, but for objective three you'll need to get stocked up. After your two days of being totally honest, you've got to go straight on to a three day drinking spree.
MOLLY	(*Surprised, raises voice*) You what?
FIONA	Buy some booze, you're going on a serious bender.
MOLLY	(*Looking horrified*) But it's against all my principles. My parents were Methodist. I signed the pledge when I was sixteen.
FIONA	You also signed a marriage certificate and look where that's got you.
MOLLY	(*Forcefully*) I've seen too many lives ruined through alcohol. It's the scourge of modern society. I can't do it.
FIONA	You know what they say. (*Forcefully*) Winners never quit. Quitters never win.
MOLLY	(*Defensively*) I can't see how getting paralytic for three days'll help my situation.
FIONA	(*Reading from book*) The author's called this chapter 'Becoming a free spirit'. The book states that drink takes the edge off things. Life looks totally different when you're inebriated.
MOLLY	(*With contempt*) I'm sure it does.
FIONA	You'll find it'll bring everything back into perspective, and change your concept of what's important in this illusion we call life. (*Looking at Molly*) Look, you've got to trust me on this one. I've been blotto many times and it makes you realize how we all get our values wrong.
MOLLY	I'm not so sure about this.

FIONA	The author states it's an essential part of the healing process. (*Putting book back into her handbag*) You're the one who's trying to get her life back together.
MOLLY	I suppose you're right. It's just that it goes against everything I believe in. (*Reluctantly*) Oh, okay, I'll give it a go.
FIONA	Who knows? You may get to enjoy it. (*Doorbell rings*)
MOLLY	(*Exits to hall – Off*) Hello, Nancy. Actually, you've caught me at a bad time, I've just …
NANCY	(*Entering from hall followed by Molly – To Fiona*) Hello, Fiona.
FIONA	Hi. (*Pause*) I really must be going.
NANCY	Don't leave on my account.
FIONA	It's all right, I've got to … um (*searching for excuse*) get to the shops. (*Walking to hall exit*) See you soon. Bye. (*Exits to hall*)
NANCY	(*Patting Molly's arm*) How are you dear? It must be difficult knowing he's just up the road in another woman's bed.
MOLLY	(*Getting cross*) Thanks for reminding me.
NANCY	Still, they say nearly half of marriages break down nowadays. I suppose I was just one of the lucky ones. Mind you, I never gave my Frank any reason to leave. (*With sorrow*) Sadly, since he's been called away to meet his maker, it's just been me and my little baby. When the time comes they're burying my little Willy with me and Frank.
MOLLY	The sooner the better. (*Searching for an explanation*) Then you'll all be together again.
NANCY	(*Looking vague*) Oh, yes. I see what you mean. (*Pause*) We've had some happy times. (*Reflectively*) I remember my little baby's cake.

MOLLY   (*Aside*) Not Willy's tenth birthday again, please.

NANCY   It was Willy's tenth birthday. I'd made him a cake and lit all the candles. Me, Frank and Willy were sitting around the table having a little chat. You'll never guess what happened next.

(*Molly now mimes what Nancy is saying*)

MOLLY   Willy unexpectedly sneezed and blew out all the NANCY candles. Me and Frank couldn't stop laughing as we tucked into that cake.

MOLLY   (*Unconvincingly*) It must have tasted delicious.

NANCY   Have you received the divorce papers yet?

MOLLY   (*Unconvincingly*) No, and there's still a chance that we could work things out.

NANCY   (*Looking surprised*) You want to be careful. Once they've strayed from the marital bed, it's difficult to ever trust them again. That Mrs Thompson's husband had five affairs. (*Discreetly*) Do you know one of them was a transsexual?

MOLLY   They say variety's the spice of life. (*Trying to get rid of Nancy*) Now I really must be getting on.

NANCY   (*Sitting down*) Don't mind me, dear. I've nothing spoiling. (*Picking up tea cup*) I could murder a cup of tea.

MOLLY   At the present time I'm rather busy. So if you don't mind, could we take a rain check on that?

NANCY   I'd have thought you'd be glad of the company. Since hubby walked out, you must be on your own quite a lot.

MOLLY   (*Indignantly*) Actually, I've been keeping myself very busy.

NANCY   (Gloating) Someone was saying your ex was in the pub last night. Apparently he was having a slap-up meal with his new lady friend. They said he was having a whale of a time. Laughing and joking all night. I guess he's making up for lost time. You never did like socialising, did you?

MOLLY	(*Getting cross*) It's not one of my favourite pastimes.
NANCY	(*With authority*) Men don't like to be suppressed. It causes them to be resentful, and that's when the trouble starts. Me and Frank did everything together. It's a pity you and your hubby hadn't any common interest. Then things might have been different.
MOLLY	(*Calmly*) Ever since we've been neighbours, I've always treated you with great respect. On many occasions I've wanted to speak the truth, but I've always held back. (*Pause*) However, there's been something I've been meaning to ask you for ages.
NANCY	(*With innocence*) What's that, my dear?
MOLLY	What causes your revolting body odour?
NANCY	(*In rage – Shouting*) You what?
MOLLY	Wherever you go, there's always the telltale smell. Is it a medical problem or a lack of personal hygiene?
NANCY	(*Getting out of the chair*) I can understand you being upset at the present time with your husband dumping you, but I don't think I've ever been so insulted in all my life.
MOLLY	Well, there's a first time for everything. And while I'm on the subject of telling the truth, people are always saying that you're one of the most boring busybodies around. Surely you must have noticed how everyone tries to avoid you.
NANCY	(*Indignantly*) I can see why your husband left you. I'll see myself out. (*Walking to hall exit*)
CLAIRE	(*Entering from hall exit with James*) Come in, Dad. You've got to see what I mean. (*To Nancy*) Oh, hello. (*Nancy walks back into room and sits on sofa. Molly exits to kitchen*)
JAMES	I don't think this was such a good idea.
CLAIRE	Wait there, Dad. I need to talk to Mum. (*Exits to kitchen*)

JAMES	(*Trying to make conversation*) It's been lovely weather lately.
NANCY	I wouldn't say that. I've been frozen. So what are you doing back here? Has your new lady friend lost interest in playing with your (*looking at James' crotch*) little magical wand?
JAMES	(*Looking embarrassed*) Actually, I've just called to have a word with my wife, in private.
NANCY	It's a bit late for that now. Let's face facts, you've been playing away from home.
JAMES	Yes, well, we can all make mistakes.
NANCY	She's much younger than you, isn't she?
JAMES	There is a slight age gap.
NANCY	I suppose she wanted to try out the more mature man. I bet you couldn't believe your luck. Posh house, money no object, flashy car, and a young nymphomaniac. You must have thought all your birthdays had arrived together.
JAMES	I don't really want to talk about it.
NANCY	Men always think that the grass is greener on the other side of the fence. Mind you, in your case, it probably was. (*With affection*) My Frank never strayed from the marital bed. He often said to me: "From the day I met you, Nancy, my life was never the same."
JAMES	(*Sarcastically*) I think I know where he was coming from.
NANCY	As the years passed, and my daughter left home, I said to Frank: "I want another baby." So he gave me Willy. (*Pause*) That dog's kept me going through troubled times.
JAMES	I'm very pleased for you.
NANCY	Dogs give unconditional love. They never let you down. I'm taking my Willy to the seaside in a couple of months. He loves swimming in the sea. I can't swim a stroke.

JAMES	(*Sarcastically*) You must be able to float. (*Aside*) You're full of hot air.
NANCY	So what were you hoping for? The best of both worlds. All the creature comforts of home, and a 'love nest' up the road.
JAMES	Nothing could be further from the truth. (*Claire and Molly enter from kitchen*)
MOLLY	(*Forcefully*) Oh, so you're still here. Actually, I think it's time you left.
JAMES	(*Assuming Molly's talking to him*) I knew this was a mistake. (*Walking to hall exit*)
MOLLY	I'm not talking to you, James. (*To Nancy*) There's no polite way to say this, so I'll come straight to the point. Would you please leave, now? I need to talk to my husband in private.
NANCY	(*Getting cross*) Well, really.
MOLLY	Yes, really.
NANCY	(*Walking to hall exit – With venom*) I'll leave you to sort out your tattered marriage. You two deserve each other. (*Exits to hall*)
MOLLY	(*With confidence*) Do you know, life's far less complicated when you actually speak your mind.
CLAIRE	Good for you, Mum.
MOLLY	(*To Claire*) I'm very cross about you asking your dad round here.
CLAIRE	(*Sitting on chair*) I'm sorry, I just thought it might help.
JAMES	Could I just say I've never seen you look so beautiful. They say you take for granted what you've already got, and I've certainly been doing that.

MOLLY	Looks are only skin deep. Why do people place so much importance on them?
JAMES	I won't be making the same mistake again. (*With sincerity*) I've learnt my lesson.
MOLLY	Right, I'm going to speak my mind. (*To Claire*) I know this may come as a shock, Claire, but I've not been put on this earth to babysit whenever you and your husband want a night out. It's probably my fault. I've spoilt you. (*Phone rings – Molly answers it*) Hello … Oh, hello, Sue … right, so you're having a get- together next Monday evening … a few drinks and nibbles. Sounds good … how kind of you to ask me … No, I'd be lying if I said I was doing anything … the thing is, I'm going to be perfectly honest with you, and please don't take this the wrong way, but I don't want to come. I don't really like these social get-togethers, they bore me to tears, although I will say the last time I came round it turned out to be quite interesting. Your husband spent all night trying to chat me up. He said he'd been dreaming about the two of us, being cast away on a desert island, skinny-dipping in the sea … Hello… Hello … (*Replaces receiver*) Oh, she's hung up.
CLAIRE	I'm not surprised.
MOLLY	Some people just can't handle the truth. (*Pause*) Now where was I? Oh, yes. (*To Claire*) All I can say is, I've done my bit for mankind, so don't expect me to be there at your beck and call. (*To James-with sadness*) Now to you, my darling husband. Over the years I've given you my life, and what thanks do I get? The minute some female shows you a bit of cleavage, you're off like a shot. You've left me in financial ruin. You've betrayed my trust. You ripped my heart out, and all for what? So that you could spend a few fleeting moments of passion between the sheets. Well, I hope you're happy. You've made your bed, now lie in it.
JAMES	(*With sincerity*) I'm so sorry. I've made the biggest mistake of my life. I want to come back.
MOLLY	(*Looking surprised*) Are you serious?

JAMES	I've never been more certain of anything in my life. Will you please take me back?

Blackout

Scene III

When the curtain rises, the stage appears to be empty. That is until Molly drags herself up from behind the sofa, with a bottle of wine in her hand. She takes a long swig from the bottle. The radio is playing 'I will survive' by Gloria Gaynor. The phone rings. Molly stands the bottle of wine on sideboard and turns the radio off. She staggers across the room in a drunken state and answers the phone.

MOLLY	(*Slurring her words*) Hello … Fiona, my darling, how are you? … I'm still partaking of the wine … I seem to be floating. I've got this warm glow inside … Yeah; my husband wants to come back … I've said I'll think about it. I've decided to finish the magical mystery tour first … The two days of telling the truth went very well, and I've still got a couple of friends left … (*Doorbell rings*) Hang on a minute, there's a ringing in my ears. Oh, it's the dumbell, don't go away, I'll get rod of them. (*Presses button on phone, puts receiver on desk and staggers through hall exit – Off*) Reverend Thomas, what the hell are you doing here? Where are you all going? (*David, Lyn, and Paul enter, followed by Molly*)
PAUL	We're here to plan out our strategy.
MOLLY	(*Holding on to a chair*) What stratosphere?
LYN	David's holding a public meeting to discuss our declining moral standards, and your daughter kindly suggested that we meet here to plan out our course of action. (*Removes her coat and puts it over a chair*)
MOLLY	(*To David*) She's not said anything to me about you becoming queer. I mean, coming here.
DAVID	(*Looking concerned*) I hope we've not called at an inconvenient time.

MOLLY	(*Unconvincingly*) Not at all. (*Staggering around the room and becoming very tactile with everyone*) I'm really pisstatic to see you all. (*With vague expression*) Welcome to my little home.
DAVID	There's something different about you Molly. You're looking positively radiant.
MOLLY	(*Seductively*) How kind of you, David, and may I say, you're looking rather fat, I mean fit. (*Arms around David*) What big biceps you have. They're so firm and round.
DAVID	(*Getting embarrassed*) Yes, well, I try and keep myself in shape. (*David moves away from Molly and gets into silent conversation with Paul. Lyn takes Molly to side of room*)
LYN	(*To Molly*) I need to have a word with you, in private. (*Looking over to David to make sure he's not listening*) Would you please do me a favour?
MOLLY	I'll do anything for you. Because I like you, (*looking thoughtful*) and I need all the friends I can get.
LYN	(*Looking bewildered*) You'll always be my friend.
MOLLY	So what flavour do you want?
LYN	(*Secretively*) Would you please give this note to David? (*Lyn hands Molly a note*)
MOLLY	Of course I will. (*Looking puzzled*) But why don't you give it to him yourself? (*Pointing to David*) Look, he's standing right over there. (*Waving to David*) Hello, David.
DAVID	(*Looking surprised*) Hello, Molly.
LYN	It's rather personal. I don't want him to read it whilst I'm here.
MOLLY	(*Looking vague*) Why not?
LYN	You know that David and I have been good friends for quite a while. I've given him so many hints that I want to take our relationship further, but he seems oblivious to my feelings. So I've decided to put my thoughts down on paper.

MOLLY	Good for you. I'll make sure he gots it.
LYN	Thank you so much. (Molly puts note on sideboard) I've just bought myself a new computer and I wanted to try it out, so I decided to kill two birds with one stone.
MOLLY	(*Looking worried*) How sad. What birds have you killed?
LYN	No, I'm speaking figuratively.
MOLLY	(*Totally confused*) Fig, what fig?
LYN	I wanted to make sure the computer wasn't going to go down on me, and at the same time let David know I wanted him to go …
MOLLY	Down on you?
LYN	(*Looking disgusted*) Certainly not. I was going to say, I wanted to invite him out for a meal. (*Pause*) Actually, I can't remember signing the note. (*Walking over to sideboard*) I'd better check.
MOLLY	I shouldn't bother. He'll know it's from you.
LYN	(*Leaving note on sideboard*) You're quite right. He's not got any other admirers.
DAVID	(*To Lyn and Molly*) We really should be getting on. (*Molly and Lyn rejoin David and Paul*)
PAUL	Actually, I can't stay too long this evening. My nephew's calling in from up north. He's going to phone me when he arrives.
MOLLY	So what moral standards are we going to be sorting out?
LYN	I'm covering chastity.
PAUL	I'll be telling people about drugs. Although I think I'm going to be a bit out of my depth.
DAVID	(*To Molly*) And of course, we've got you down to talk on the perils of alcohol.

MOLLY	(*Looking at all the bottles of drink*) Dear Lord, I forgot about the drink.
	(*Molly staggers over to bottles of drink. She takes a cloth from the drawer and unseen by anyone, she throws it over the bottles*)
DAVID	We're relying on you to expound the virtues of sobriety. We can't let things go on the way they are.
LYN	Your daughter was telling me you signed the pledge at sixteen and spent a lifetime in total abstinence.
MOLLY	(*Looking guilty*) I've not had a drip, and that's the Cod's honest tooth.
DAVID	So you, more than anyone, can speak with conviction. You're a shining example to the rest of us.
MOLLY	(*Looking into David's eyes*) Oh, David, you are a sweetie. (*Almost throwing up*) Actually, I'm not feeling too well. (*Moving away from David*)
DAVID	(*With concern*) Oh, dear. Nothing serious, I hope?
LYN	You could be in for a viral infection. I know quite a few people who've been struck down.
MOLLY	I think a black coffee might help. (*Getting agitated*) Anyone care to join me?
LYN	Yes, please. (*Lyn, Paul and David place their orders in quick succession*) White, without sugar.
PAUL	Black, one sugar, please.
DAVID	Same for me but no sugar, thank you.
MOLLY	(*Looking bewildered*) So that's … Three back … Two wine … No hang on a minute. … Um …
DAVID	I'll tell you what, Molly, make them all black, then bring in the milk and sugar and we can all help ourselves.

MOLLY	(*To David*) I can see why you're in charge of the flock. I won't be long, feel free to start the meeting without me. I'm going to plop in the kitchen. (*Molly staggers through the kitchen exit – Everyone takes a seat*)
PAUL	Is Molly all right? She's acting rather strange tonight.
LYN	It's probably the result of the marital breakdown.
DAVID	We must make allowances. Her world's been turned upside down.
LYN	I feel so sorry for her. (*Getting cross*) Some men can be real swines. (*Getting embarrassed*) Please forgive me, David. It's just that I get so cross when men can't control their sexual urges.
PAUL	It's not always down to the man. You can't fit a masonry screw without a rawlplug.
LYN	I haven't got a clue what you're on about. All I know is, on several occasions, I've been aware of married men lustfully looking and mentally undressing me.
PAUL	The mind boggles.
DAVID	(*Looking at his watch*) I think it's time we began the meeting. Let's start with a short prayer. (*Everyone bows their heads*) Dear Lord, grant me the serenity to accept the things I cannot change. The courage to change the things I can, and the wisdom to know the difference. Amen.
PAUL	Could I kick off by saying? …
DAVID	I suggest we have a few moments of silence to allow that still small voice to speak to us.

(*Everyone sits in silence with their heads bowed*)

| FIONA | (*On speaker phone*) Hello … Is anyone there? |
| LYN | (*Looking upward*) It's divine intervention. We're witnessing a miracle. |

FIONA	(*On speaker phone*) Please speak to me.
DAVID	Actually, I'm not so sure that's a voice from above. (*Looking at phone*) I think it's coming from that phone. (*Walking over to phone and picking up receiver*) Hello.
FIONA	(*On speaker phone*) Where's Molly?
DAVID	She's in the kitchen making a coffee. This is the Reverend David Thomas. We're holding a meeting here to discuss the possibility of reaching into the community to improve our moral standards. Molly's very kindly agreed to talk on the total abstinence from alcohol.
FIONA	(*On speaker phone*) That should be interesting. (*Pause*) Best of luck. Tell Molly I'll ring her later. Bye.
DAVID	(*Switching off phone and replacing receiver*) Molly must have inadvertently switched the phone on to speaker mode. (*Returning to his seat*) Now, where were we?
PAUL	As I was saying, I'm not so sure about my role on the drug scene. I mean, say someone starts asking awkward questions?
LYN	You must turn to the Lord for guidance. He'll point them in the right direction.
PAUL	Everyone on my estate knows the right direction. The dealer only lives at the end of my street.
DAVID	It's important that we let people know that God cares for them.
LYN	(*Condescendingly*) My thoughts exactly, David. (*Seductively*) You always seem to know what's going on in my mind.
DAVID	Well, it's good to know we're on the same wavelength.
LYN	(*Seductively – smiling at David*) So what do you suggest we do about it?

DAVID   (*Oblivious to advances*) We've got to challenge people. We've got to make them face up to the reality of life. (Lyn looks disappointed) As humans, we encounter all the temptations that the world has to offer, and being frail, we need help to overcome them.

LYN   I fervently believe in the subject you've given me, David. My body's not being defiled by some man seeking the pleasures of the flesh.

DAVID   I will say that marriage seems to have lost its meaning.

LYN   Respect and dignity are a thing of the past. We're living in a society where free love seems to be the norm.

PAUL   I've never been offered any free love.

(*Doorbell rings*)

LYN   I'll go. Molly's obviously busy. (*Exits to hall – Off*) Oh, hello, Nancy.

NANCY   (*Off*) Is the vicar here?

LYN   (*Off*) Yes, he is.

NANCY   (*Entering from hall with Lyn*) I need to talk to him, urgently. (*Crying uncontrollably*) Oh, Vicar, you've got to help me. Someone's run over Willy.

DAVID   (*Standing up and putting his arms around Nancy*) Calm down, Nancy. What's happened?

(*Molly staggers in from kitchen carrying a tray with cups of coffee, some milk and a bowl of sugar. She is spilling it everywhere*)

NANCY   (*To David*) My little baby was relieving himself on the back wheel of a double-decker bus when the driver put it into reverse and drove over him.

DAVID   (*With concern*) Oh dear. Was he injured?

NANCY   (*Crying hysterically*) He's dead. When they gave him to me, he was as flat as a pancake.

DAVID	How absolutely awful.
NANCY	By the time I'd got home, he was as stiff as a board. (*Crying unconsolably*)
DAVID	There, there, try not to upset yourself.
LYN	One thing's for sure, he wouldn't have felt any pain.
MOLLY	(*Trying to sound sympathetic*) That's right. It was all over in a slash. I mean flash. (*Pause*) Why don't you get stuffed?
NANCY	(*Looking bewildered*) YOU WHAT? (*Stops crying*)
MOLLY	Take Willy to a taxi … taxider … Put him in a taxi and take him to a shop where they can stuff him.
NANCY	I couldn't do that.
DAVID	(*With concern*) I suppose you want to remember him as he was.
NANCY	No, it's just that he's been completely flattened. He's like a dinner plate. (*Molly hands tray of coffee to Nancy, then exits to kitchen*) I'll never forgive myself. It's all my fault.
LYN	(*Sympathetically*) Of course it isn't.
NANCY	He wanted to relieve himself in the park, but I was in a hurry to catch the bus. That last look on his little face when he was finally able to spend a penny will haunt me for the rest of my life. He was going to be sixteen next Tuesday. (*Crying*) He'll never get to open his presents now. (*Handing tray of coffee to David*)
DAVID	(*Looking upward*) You've got to realise, he's gone to a better place. (*Handing tray of coffee to Paul*)
NANCY	(*Stops crying*) Only last week we sat together and watched a party political broadcast. I'm sure he understood every word the Prime Minister was saying.
PAUL	He must have been the only one who did. (*Handing tray of coffee to Lyn*)

DAVID	Molly's just making us all a coffee. Why don't you join us?
NANCY	(*With self-pity*) I don't want to impose myself on anyone.
DAVID	Of course you're not imposing. (*Pause*) How do you like it?
NANCY	White, two sugars, please.
LYN	I'll tell Molly. (*Exits to kitchen with tray of spilled coffee*)
NANCY	Willy was such an obedient dog. Frank took him for training when he was a pup. I only had to blow the whistle and he'd come running.
PAUL	Who, Frank?
NANCY	He was always doing little tricks. His favourite one was to stand on his back legs begging for me to throw him a biscuit. Once I accidentally threw Frank's lighter at him. My Frank had to wait three days before he could have a cigarette. (*With sorrow*) That lighter's got pride of place on my mantelpiece. It's my memorial to Frank and Willy.
DAVID	I suggest you sit down for a few minutes. We're having a get together to plan a public meeting where we're going to be discussing our declining moral standards. We're covering several subjects. Lyn's on chastity.
PAUL	I'm on the drugs.
LYN	(*Entering from kitchen*) Molly's on the toilet. (**Pause**) She's being sick. (*Nancy sits on a chair*)
DAVID	Oh, dear. She must have caught that viral infection you were on about, Lyn.
LYN	I'll make some more coffee. Won't be a sec. (*Exits to kitchen. - Paul's mobile phone rings*)
PAUL	Excuse me. (*Speaking into his mobile phone*) Hello … Oh, hello, Phil … Where are you? … At my house. But you said you wouldn't be arriving till ten … I can't

put them all up … All right, I'll sort something out … See you in a minute … Bye. (*Switches off mobile phone*) I'm sorry but I've got to go. My nephew's arrived with four of his rugby mates. They're all wanting somewhere to sleep tonight.

DAVID   Oh dear. It looks as though we'll need to reconvene the meeting for another time.

NANCY   I've got a couple of spare beds if that's any use.

PAUL   That's very kind of you, Nancy.

DAVID   I'm sure Lyn's got a spare bed at her house.

PAUL   Been checking in her bedroom, David?

DAVID   (*Getting embarrassed*) Certainly not. I'll go and ask her if she can help. (*Exits to kitchen*)

PAUL   I'll give you a lift home in my car if that's all right.
Then we can drop a couple of the lads at your place.
(*Pause*) I greatly appreciate this, Nancy.

NANCY   I'll be glad of the company. (*With great sadness*) My house is like a morgue at the moment.

PAUL   How do you think the new vicar's settling in?

NANCY   He seems very nice. I'm sure he'll fit in well.

PAUL   The only thing is, at thirty-five I'm surprised he's not married. (*Looking thoughtful*) Perhaps he's gay.

NANCY   My Frank was forty when we got married, (*with lustful intent*) and I can assure you there was nothing gay about him.

PAUL   I guess he just enjoys the freedom of being single. I suppose being the vicar he gets all the women pouring out their hearts, which gives him the opportunity of chatting them up.

NANCY   You've got that wrong. I've been alone with him several times and he's never made any amorous advances towards me. (*Pause*) I think you'll find he's just a quiet, shy, unassuming gentleman.

(David enters from kitchen carrying Lyn's blouse. Lyn follows looking embarrassed)

PAUL   What were you saying, Nancy? (*To David*) The idea was to see if Lyn's got a spare bed. Not take her to bed.

DAVID   (*Handing Lyn her blouse*) You don't understand. (*Defensively*) Please tell them what happened, Lyn.

LYN   Molly's being sick everywhere. She's just thrown up all over my blouse.

DAVID   Lyn's removed it to rinse it through.

PAUL   We believe you, thousands wouldn't. (*To Lyn*) Is there any chance of putting my nephew's friend up?

LYN   No problem at all. I've got the spare bed all made up.

DAVID   I suggest we meet after the service on Sunday and fix another date for our get together.

PAUL   Sorry about this.

DAVID   I'd better explain to Molly what's going on.

LYN   (*Putting her coat on*) See you tomorrow, David.

PAUL   Apologise to Molly for me. Bye.
             (*Paul, Nancy and Lyn exit to hall. David sorts out some paperwork. Molly staggers in from kitchen*)

MOLLY   Where is everyone? (*Looking behind the sofa*)

DAVID   There's been an unexpected turn in events. Everyone's had to leave.

MOLLY   Don't tell me Willy's risen from the dead?

DAVID   Unfortunately not. Paul needs some youngsters put up for the night. So everyone's sorting out beds.

MOLLY   (*Looking vague*) Oh right. (*Pause*) By the way, I've got a note for you, David. (*Hands over Lyn's note*) I can't remember turning the bathroom tap off. Won't be a sec. (*Staggers through kitchen exit*)

DAVID (*Reading aloud from note*) Dear David, Recently I've been giving a lot of thought to the two of us. Bearing in mind my present circumstances, I would like to ask you out for a meal to talk about our future together. You must have noticed that over the past few months the affection I have towards you has grown, and without wishing to seem presumptuous, I'd like to move things on. (*Looking up from the note and talking aloud*) I never realized Molly had any feelings towards me. (*Molly enters from kitchen*) You're certainly a dark horse, Molly. (*Holding up note*) I'll need to give this some serious thought.

MOLLY (*Thinking he is talking about Lyn*) Well, don't take too long. (*Stroking David's arm*) Girls don't wait around for ever.

DAVID I've always been quite shy when it comes to members of the opposite sex.

MOLLY I don't believe that.

DAVID (*Fiddling with his clerical collar*) It's true. I've never been much of a ladies' man.

MOLLY I can't see why. (*Getting close*) You're articulated, good-looking and you've got lovely thighs, eyes.

DAVID You're a beautiful woman, Molly. Your husband must have been foolish leaving you.

MOLLY (*Clinging hold of David*) Can you help me, David? (*Crying uncontrollably*) I lay in bed at night longing to be free of my nightwear, I mean nightmare.

DAVID (*Handing Molly his handkerchief*) There, there, try not to upset yourself. (*Molly blows her nose on the handkerchief and hands it back to David*)

MOLLY (*Stops crying*) Thank you. If only I'd met someone like you years ago.

DAVID Well, who knows what the future holds. Let's leave it in the Lord's hands.

MOLLY	You're quite right, David. (*Pause*) So, getting back to the note, you will give it some thought?
DAVID	Of course I will. (*Seductively*) Life certainly has a few unexpected twists and turns. I really must be going. See you soon, Molly. (*David exits to hall – The phone rings. Molly answers it – Slurring her words*)
MOLLY	Hello … Sorry? … I haven't got a clue who you are … Oh, I see, so you're that nice young man at the health spa who gave me a massage every day? … (*In a sexy voice*) Hello Steve, how are you? … Pardon? … You want to take me out for dinner? … But I'm old enough to be your moth … older sister, you naughty boy … All right, yes, that sounds very rice … I'll tell you what, leave me your number and I'll ring you … Just a minute, let me get a pen … (*Staggers across to drawer and returns to phone with a pen*) Right, I'm all yours … (*Writes down number*) 07815, slow down … 683586 … Okay, I'll be in touch … Bye. (*Replaces receiver. Doorbell rings – Molly staggers through hall exit – Off*) What are you doing here? (*Entering from hall with James – who is carrying a suitcase*)
JAMES	I've moved out, and I've nowhere to go. (*In desperation*) Please forgive me and take me back?

Blackout

ACT II

Scene I

When the curtain rises, Fiona and Claire are sitting down talking.

CLAIRE   I'd like to know what's going on.

FIONA   What do you mean?

CLAIRE   Surely you must have noticed Mum's behaviour's been rather strange recently.

FIONA   (*Trying to look innocent*) Actually, I can't say that I have.

CLAIRE   Well, you're the only one who hasn't. Firstly she spends six hundred quid at a health spa. Then, she starts upsetting all her friends. One of them asked Mum what she thought of her new hairstyle, and Mum said it reminded her of a wet floor mop. If that wasn't enough, for the past three days she's been on another planet. If I didn't know better, I'd have said she'd been on the booze.

FIONA   (*Unconvincingly*) We both know your mum's never touched a drop of alcohol in her life.

CLAIRE   (*Looking horrified*) You don't think she's started on the drugs, do you? With Dad clearing off, who knows what she's capable of doing?

FIONA   Your mum's one of the most well-balanced, sensible people I know.

CLAIRE   If only we could turn the clock back and stop all this from happening.

FIONA   If life were predictable, it would be boring.

CLAIRE   I was listening to a programme on the radio yesterday. Apparently, infidelity in men is caused by a lack of blood. There's not enough to supply their brains and the bits below at the same time. So the minute a man starts getting amorous, all the blood drains from his brain and flows to the nether regions. Thus rendering him incapable of making any rational decisions.

FIONA	That explains a lot of things.
CLAIRE	So, getting back to Mum, are you sure you're telling me everything?
FIONA	(*Unconvincingly*) You know as much as I do. (*Pause*) What's happening about your dad? I believe he's staying with you?
CLAIRE	He hadn't got anywhere else to go. Mum said she wasn't ready to have him back. Which reminds me, I'd better get home and get the dinner organised.
FIONA	I'm sure they'll work things out fairly soon.
CLAIRE	I wish I had your confidence. (*Walking to hall exit*) Parents, who'd have them? (*Exits to hall*)
FIONA	(*Dials number on her mobile phone*) Hello, it's me … You know you said you were going to become a blood donor tonight. Forget it … I'll explain when you get home … See you later, love you lots … Bye. (*Switches off her mobile phone. Molly enters from Kitchen*)
MOLLY	Where's Claire?
FIONA	She's just popped back home. (*Pause*) So how are things at the moment? Have you binned all the booze?
MOLLY	No, I've decided to keep a few bottles of red wine. I've acquired quite a taste for it. You were right when you said that it brings everything back into perspective.
FIONA	So what about your lecture on the perils of alcohol? (*Getting book from handbag and reading it*)
MOLLY	I'll be like the politicians. Do as I say, not as I do.
FIONA	How's the Marital merry-go-round going?
MOLLY	When you first told me about it, I thought, what a waste of time, but it's really helping me.
FIONA	There was an article in the paper last week. Apparently it's proving to be the greatest rescue remedy for women of this century.

MOLLY	I'm just aiming to get my life sorted.
FIONA	So you're ready to move on to objective number four. (*Reading from book*) The author's called this chapter 'Becoming proactive and not reactive'.
MOLLY	(*Looking vague*) What's that supposed to mean?
FIONA	It's quite simple really. You've got to take command of a situation. For objective four, you've only got to do one thing. Kiss the first man who walks through your door.
MOLLY	Is that all? This'll be a doddle.
FIONA	Just two things to remember. It's got to be within one minute of him entering, and it can't just be a peck on the cheek. This kiss has got to be one he's going to remember for the rest of his life.
MOLLY	(*Looking stunned*) I'm a respectable middle-aged woman. Well, I was until two weeks ago. I can't just accost the first male who walks in here.
FIONA	What were you saying a minute ago about your life being on the up? That's all due to the Marital merry-go-round. (*Pause*) The author states that women must be in control of their own destiny. These challenges are all about restoring your lost confidence. Most women passively wait for the man to make the first move. (*Putting book back into her handbag*) Well, now it's your turn to take the initiative with a random male.
MOLLY	I could be had up for molestation. (*Pause*) Oh, well, I've come this far. I might as well go all the way.
FIONA	That's the spirit. I hear your husband's moved out of his love nest.
MOLLY	Yes, I was tempted to take him back, then I thought, no, I'll let him suffer a bit longer.
FIONA	Will you take him back, eventually?
MOLLY	A couple of weeks ago I'd have said no, but as the days pass, I realize how much I miss him. We've been through too much together to throw it all away.

FIONA	So what about his passionate fling?
MOLLY	Like you were saying the other day. His brains have been wired up wrong. Everything short circuits at the sight of a pretty female.
FIONA	I get the feeling you're well on the road to recovery. (*Walking to hall exit*) I'll leave you to it. Bye. (*Exits to hall – Molly checks that Fiona has gone. She then dials number on phone*)
MOLLY	Hello, James, it's me … I want you to get round here now. I need your help with something … Great, I'll see you in a minute. (*Replaces receiver – Doorbell rings. Molly exits to hall – Off*) Fiona, is that you?
DAVID	(*Off*) No, it's the Reverent Thomas. May I come in?
MOLLY	(*Shouting – Off*) Could you pop back a bit later? It's not very convenient at the moment.
DAVID	(*Off*) I just need to speak with you for a minute.
MOLLY	(*Entering from hall*) I can't face anyone right now.
DAVID	(*Off*) Whatever's happened, Molly?
MOLLY	Nothing's happened. I just need to be left alone.
DAVID	(*Off*) It's my duty to help in times like this. I'm not going anywhere till you've told me what's wrong. I suggest we have a short time of meditation together. (*Pause*) Molly, I'm coming in.
MOLLY	No, you mustn't. (*David enters carrying a bible*)
DAVID	There's no need to be distressed. The Bible has the answers to all our problems.
MOLLY	That's reassuring to hear.
DAVID	Actually, when we had our get together the other evening, I did sense you weren't quite yourself.
MOLLY	Yes, well. Things have been a bit fraught lately.

DAVID	I need you to pour out your heart. (*Placing bible on table*) Nothing you can say or do would shock me.
MOLLY	We'll soon find out. (*Looking at her watch*) Is that the time?
DAVID	Have you got to go somewhere?
MOLLY	No, I'm all yours.
DAVID	Talking of which, I've been reading the note you gave me. Actually, I've read it over and over again. It's caused me some sleepless nights. In fact, I've been praying about it on several occasions.
MOLLY	(*Seductively*) You know what they say, when love's on offer, you've got to grab it with both hands.
DAVID	(*Molly grabs David and gives him a passionate kiss. She then removes his jacket. She continues to kiss and cuddle him*) What the? … Good grief … (*Tries to compose himself*) Molly, what are you doing? (*Molly grabs David and goes into another passionate kiss – David is totally dishevelled*) Please remember, I'm a man of the cloth … I feel a sermon coming on. (*David removes his shirt and clerical collar. The doorbell rings*)
MOLLY	That'll be my husband.
DAVID	I think we both need to start praying, for guidance.
MOLLY	It's too late to be praying for guidance. Go to my bedroom. I'll be up in a minute.
DAVID	The Bishop's not going to like this.
MOLLY	The Bishop's not going to be getting it.

(*David rushes through hall exit. Molly hides his jacket, shirt and clerical collar out of sight, behind a chair. She then exits to hall – Off*)

	Steve, what are you doing here? I said I'd ring you at the health spa
STEVE	(*Off*) I couldn't wait any longer. (*Entering from hall, followed by Molly*) I just had to see you.

MOLLY	Look, we don't know anything about each other. I'm a married woman.
STEVE	You told me your husband had left you. You said that your life had fallen apart.
MOLLY	The thing is, when you're having a massage, you tend to pour out your heart.
STEVE	(*Sensually*) Why don't I give you a massage now? I could work on that sofa. (*Pointing at sofa*)
MOLLY	I don't think that's the best of ideas. My husband'll be here any minute.
STEVE	In that case, let's not waste time. (*Starting to rub Molly's neck*) When you were at the health spa, this is what you enjoyed most.
MOLLY	Aren't you like a doctor? Didn't you sign a Hippocratic Oath not to mix business with pleasure? (*Steve continues rubbing Molly's neck*) Would you please stop doing that?
STEVE	Don't you like it?
MOLLY	I love it. That's why you've got to stop. (*Moving away from Steve*) Look, in case you hadn't noticed, there is a slight age gap between us.
STEVE	So what? I'm looking for a lady with a bit of class and experience. Someone who knows what's going on in the world, and you tick all the right boxes.
MOLLY	Yes, well, I'm very flattered. However, my life's a bit complicated at the moment. (*Pause*) Give me a few days to sort things out. Then I'll be in touch. (*Pause*) Now, you really must go.
STEVE	You said you'd ring me, but you didn't. You're nothing but a little tease. Actually, that's what I like about you. Most girls throw themselves at me.
MOLLY	That's one thing I won't be doing.

STEVE	I'll make a deal with you. One kiss, and then I'll leave.
MOLLY	(*Looking shocked*) You've got to be joking. (*Unconvincingly*) I'm not in the habit of kissing men who've just walked through my door.
STEVE	A few days ago I had my hands all over your naked body. So what's changed?
MOLLY	That was in the line of duty.
STEVE	As my mum used to say, "There's nowt for the dumb in this world."
MOLLY	Well, tell your mum that her son's a bit too forward for my liking.
STEVE	(*With sorrow*) I can't. She passed away a couple of years ago. She's left a real gap in my life.
MOLLY	I'm very sorry to hear that, but I'm not going to be your surrogate mother.
STEVE	I'm only asking for one little kiss. (*Persuasively*) This is the twenty-first century.
MOLLY	Don't you ever take no for an answer?
STEVE	I've travelled nearly fifty miles to see you. So what do you say?
MOLLY	So, it's one kiss? Then you promise you'll leave?
STEVE	Yes, I promise.
MOLLY	(*Offering her cheek*) Oh, all right.
STEVE	(*Kissing Molly passionately*) Now we're getting somewhere. (*Kissing Molly again*)
MOLLY	Stop. Stop. (*In a state of shock*) You should be forced to carry a government health warning. My blood pressure's just gone through the roof.
JAMES	(*Off*) Hello. It's me.

49

MOLLY	Oh no. (*Pushing Steve towards kitchen exit*) It's my husband. Go in there. I'll shout when it's clear. (*Pushing Steve through kitchen exit. Molly tries to compose herself*)
JAMES	(*Entering from hall*) So, what did you want?
MOLLY	(*Searching for an excuse*) Um … I need to borrow a fiver.
JAMES	(*With disappointment*) Oh, is that all? (*Handing over a fiver*) I thought you may have changed your mind about us.
MOLLY	Not at the moment.
JAMES	Oh, right. Why don't I make us both a tea? (*Getting close to Molly*) Then we can have a proper chat about our future.
MOLLY	(*Moving away*) It's not very convenient at the moment. (*Standing in front of kitchen exit*)
JAMES	Look, I've been a fool. I can only say sorry. It'll never happen again. I'd swear that in front of the vicar if he was here.
MOLLY	Really?
JAMES	What have you been doing with yourself today?
MOLLY	(*Unconvincingly*) Oh, nothing much. It's been quite boring.
JAMES	Now I'm here, could we pop up to the bedroom?
MOLLY	(*Getting cross*) You've got a nerve.
JAMES	You don't understand. I'm running low on shirts, and I've got some spare ones in the wardrobe. (*Walking to hall exit*)
MOLLY	(*Searching for an excuse*) Not any more. I've given them all to Oxfam. (*Standing in front of hall exit*)

JAMES	How about my charcoal suit?
MOLLY	That went as well.
JAMES	Don't worry, I never did like it.
MOLLY	(*Getting cross*) I bought you that one.
JAMES	(*Looking guilty*) Thinking about it, that was the only one I did like. (*Pause*) What can I do to convince you that I'm truly sorry? If I could see my time again, I wouldn't make the same mistake.

(*Doorbell rings. Molly walks to hall exit*)

MOLLY	This is like Piccadilly Circus in here. (*Exits to hall – Off*) Lyn, what are you doing?
LYN	(*Entering from hall, followed by Molly*) I need to know what David's reaction was to my note. (*Spotting James*) Oh, hello.
JAMES	Hi.
LYN	Sorry, am I interrupting anything?
MOLLY	(*Looking at watch*) No, James was just leaving.
JAMES	But I've only just got here. (*There is a crashing sound from upstairs*) What was that?
MOLLY	(*Unconvincingly*) I didn't hear anything.
LYN	You must have. It sounded like someone falling over in the bedroom. It could be a burglar.
JAMES	(*Walking to hall exit*) I'll have a quick look. Best to be on the safe side. (*Exits to hall*)
MOLLY	(*Calling to James*) There's no need. It won't be anything.
LYN	So tell me what David said about my note?
MOLLY	He said he'd been praying for guidance, and when he wasn't praying he's been tossing and turning in his bed thinking about you.

LYN	(*Looking pleased*) It sounds as though I've started things moving.
MOLLY	(*Looking at her watch*) Yes, well, I'll keep you up to speed. (*Walking to hall exit*) It's been nice talking to you.
LYN	Would you like me to call when it's more convenient?
MOLLY	That would be much better.
LYN	Are you all right now? Only when we called the other evening, you were feverish and being sick.
MOLLY	I'm fine now, thanks. Sorry about your blouse.
LYN	Don't give it a second thought. (*Walking to hall exit*) Oh, by the way, have you seen Nancy lately? I've never seen such a change in anyone. She's become subdued and very polite. (*Pause*) And what's more, there was always a slight odour when she was around. Well, it's gone.
JAMES	(*Entering from hall with David*) I've just found the vicar in your bedroom.
LYN	David, what's going on? Why are you in a state of undress?
DAVID	There's a very simple explanation to this.
LYN	(*Getting cross*) So, what is it?
DAVID	Well … Um … You see …
STEVE	(*Entering from kitchen – Holding mobile phone in his hand*) I've had a call from work, they need me back there urgently. (*To Molly*) So what's my chance of a night out?
JAMES	Night out?
LYN	David, I'm waiting for an explanation.
JAMES	So am I.
MOLLY	Does anyone fancy a cup of tea?

Blackout

Scene II

When the curtain rises, Fiona is sitting on the sofa, and Molly is sitting on a chair.

MOLLY   I must admit, it was rather embarrassing.

FIONA   I think you did very well convincing everyone that it was all totally innocent.

MOLLY   (*Looking ashamed*) I've never told so many lies in my whole life. (*Pause*) I said that the vicar had been stung by a bee. So he'd removed his clothes and went upstairs to get rid of the sting. Then I told everyone that Steve was a plumber fixing a leaking tap, and I was treating him to a meal as payment.

FIONA   I'm well impressed.

MOLLY   Fortunately, the vicar decided to take a vow of silence, so didn't compromise my story. And Steve was called back to the health spa before anyone could quiz him about the joys of being a plumber.

FIONA   (*With relish*) So, what's it like having a toy boy?

MOLLY   A bit scary. Nothing like this has ever happened to me before.

FIONA   That just goes to prove how you've turned your life around.

MOLLY   I have to say, there's something exciting about a frisky young man having the hots for you.

FIONA   (*Seriously*) You realize he's at his sexual peak.

MOLLY   You don't need to tell me. I nearly suffered a cardiac arrest after our last encounter.

FIONA   Think of all that pent-up energy waiting to be expelled. (*Looking thoughtful*) Has he got any brothers?

MOLLY   Actually, I'm too old for all this sort of thing.

FIONA	The only time you're too old is when you're in your box. (*Pause*) So, what's happened since you kissed the vicar?
MOLLY	This might sound stupid, but I think he's got a crush on me. (*Looking thoughtful*) Even before I gave him the kiss he was acting rather strange.
FIONA	There's nothing more desirable than a defenceless, vulnerable woman facing the world on her own.
MOLLY	I'm sure it's totally innocent. Lyn's the girl who's got her eyes set on the vicar.
	(*Doorbell rings. Molly exits to hall*)
NANCY	(*Off*) Sorry to bother you. Could I have a word please?
MOLLY	(*Off*) Yes, come in.
	(*Molly enters, followed by Nancy who is wearing a brightly coloured Lycra outfit and cycle helmet*)
NANCY	Oh, hello, Fiona.
FIONA	(*Staring at Nancy*) Don't tell me you've started playing water polo?
NANCY	No, nothing like that. (*Pause*) I decided I needed a new interest, so I've joined a cycling club for the over fifties. We're not out to break any speed records. We just enjoy meandering through the countryside, observing the wildlife.
FIONA	(*Unconvincingly*) Sounds like a real barrel of laughs.
NANCY	Paul's joined as well. (*Taking Molly to side of room away from Fiona*) I need to have a word in private. (*Aside - to Molly*) The real reason for my visit is to say, thank you, (*Fiona gets the Marital merry-go-round from her handbag and reads it*) for telling me a few home truths. I've been giving a lot of thought to what you said the other day.
MOLLY	I'm sorry about that. I was totally out of order.

NANCY   Not at all. I'm glad you spoke out. (*Pause*) After Frank
              passed on I became quite bitter. I was insensitive to
              people's feelings. But after listening to you, I realized I
              needed to change my ways. (*Nancy looks at Fiona who
              is still reading the book. She whispers to Molly*) There's
              one more thing you could do for me. Would you tell me
              if I've still got any personal hygiene problems?

MOLLY   (*Sniffing*) No, you're absolutely fine.

NANCY   What a relief. Thank you. (*Looking at watch*) Is that the
              time? (*Walking over to Fiona*) I must dash. We're going
              for a ride to the Spyglass and Kettle for a light snack.

FIONA   Don't get drunk.

NANCY   There's no chance of that. The vicar's going to be joining
              us.

FIONA   (*Sarcastically*) You've always been teetotal, haven't you,
              Molly?

(*Molly glares at Fiona*)

NANCY   Nice to see you both. Bye. (*Nancy exits to hall*)

FIONA   What was all that about?

MOLLY   She was one of my victims during the forty-eight hour
              truth telling challenge. I pointed out that she was a
              busybody with body odour.

FIONA   I'm amazed she's still speaking to you.

MOLLY   She's just thanked me for what I did.

FIONA   I'm very impressed with your resolve in tackling the
              Marital merry-go-round. When you started, I thought
              you'd soon give up, but I've been proved totally wrong.

MOLLY   I had nothing to lose. (*With sincerity*) My life had reached
              rock bottom.

FIONA   So it's on to the penultimate step. (*Reading from the
              book*) This is where things get a bit more serious.

MOLLY	I don't like the sound of this.
FIONA	You're now going to push the boundaries to the limit. For this challenge you've got to give yourself to the first man you share a romantic meal with.
MOLLY	(*Looking horrified*) Are you saying what I think you're saying? I've got to make love to some man who buys me a meal?
FIONA	That's right.
MOLLY	I'm going to be way out of my depth on this one. (*Pause*) Whatever's the author's thinking behind such an objective?
FIONA	It's now time to shed all your inhibitions, and prove to yourself that you're a real woman with sex appeal. To do this you must seduce your dinner date.
MOLLY	They've always said. "There's no such thing as a free lunch." (*Looking thoughtful*) Actually, this is going to be easy. I've invited James round for a chat about our future. I'll talk him into taking me out for a meal tonight. We'll come home and re-consummate our marriage and get our lives back to some form of normality.
FIONA	(*Putting book back into her handbag*) I'm not sure that's what the author had in mind. Still, I suppose as long as you complete the six steps, you'll be fine.
JAMES	(*Off*) Hello.
MOLLY	Talk of the devil. (*Shouting to hall exit*) Come in. Fiona's here.
JAMES	(*Entering from hall*) Hello. (*To Fiona*) I've been meaning to say a big thank you for helping Molly through these last few months, while I've been acting like an idiot.
FIONA	Not a problem. (*Pause*) I'll leave you to it. (*Walking to hall exit*) Have a great time tonight. Bye. (*Exits to hall*)
JAMES	She's been a good friend to you.

MOLLY	More than you'll ever know. If it hadn't been for Fiona's help, I'm not sure I'd have got through all this.
JAMES	So, how are you?
MOLLY	(*Looking thoughtful*) Five months ago my life was ticking along fairly smoothly. Then you turned my world upside down. (*Sternly*) How could you put me through all this?
JAMES	I don't know what I can say or do to make amends. Call it the mid-life crisis. In the cold light of day, it sounds pathetic. All I can say is that it will never happen again.
MOLLY	Too damn right it won't. There's going to be no second chance here. You've used your one and only lifeline.
JAMES	Can't I phone a friend? Only joking.
MOLLY	(*Getting cross*) Oh, very funny.
JAMES	Over the last few days, you've changed. I can't put my finger on it, but you're like a new woman.
MOLLY	A lot of things have happened over the last few days.
JAMES	Will you forgive me? I'll do anything to make amends.
MOLLY	You can start by showing me a bit of attention. I want you to make me feel special.
JAMES	Let's go out for an evening together. Like a first date.
MOLLY	Sounds good to me. There's a new restaurant opening in town. How about …?
JAMES	I've got the perfect answer. We spent all our first dates in the cinema. Let's recapture those magical, romantic moments by going to see a movie.
MOLLY	Actually, I'd rather … (*Phone rings – Molly answers it*) Hello … Oh, hello, Claire … Yes, your dad's here … Oh, right, so you've both got to go … I'm sure your dad'll look after him. (*To James*) Claire needs you to babysit for a while. They've got to go to the solicitors, now.

JAMES	But what about our chat?
MOLLY	Call round tomorrow, we'll talk then.
JAMES	All right, tell her I'm on my way. Bye. (*James gives Molly a peck on the cheek. Then he exits to kitchen*)
MOLLY	(*Speaking into phone*) He'll be there in a minute ... Claire, I need you to persuade your father to take me for a meal instead of going to the pictures ... Right, that's great ... Speak to you soon ... Bye. (*Replaces receiver – Doorbell rings. Molly exits to hall – Off*) Hello, Lyn, come in.

(*Lyn and Molly enter from hall*)

LYN	I'm sorry to bother you, but I'm worried about David.
MOLLY	Why, what's happened?
LYN	Nothing, that's the problem. Ever since you gave him my note, he's been quite distant. In fact, it's almost as though it's put him off me.
MOLLY	You're worrying unnecessarily. He was overwhelmed by it. He's told me so on several occasions.
LYN	(*Looking puzzled*) How strange. He's never mentioned it to me. I don't like to phone and book a meal. What do you think I should do?
MOLLY	I'm the last person to ask anything about a relationship. What goes on in a man's brain is one of the unsolved mysteries of the universe. (*Pause*) I'll tell you what, why don't I make us both a cup of tea? Then we can have a chat about your options.
LYN	That would be lovely. (*Pause*) I can't remember locking my car. I'll just check. (*Lyn exits to hall and Molly exits to kitchen. After a few seconds Lyn, David and Paul enter from hall*) Come in. Molly's in the kitchen.
MOLLY	(*Entering from kitchen*) David, Paul, how nice to see you. This is an unexpected pleasure.

PAUL	Hello, Molly. We're here on a mission.
DAVID	(*To Lyn*) I'm so pleased you're here, Lyn. We've got a little surprise for you.
LYN	Sounds interesting. Well, don't keep me in suspense. What is it?
DAVID	You tell her, Paul.
PAUL	There's a new restaurant opening in town tonight. My son's going to be the head chef. He's given me a complimentary voucher. It's for a table for four.
DAVID	(*To Lyn*) Would you please join me tonight for an evening out?
LYN	(*Ecstatically*) I'd love to. Thank you.
MOLLY	(*To David and Paul*) We're just having a cup of tea. Would you both like one?
DAVID	We're not quite finished yet. (*Pause*) Let's do this together, Paul.
PAUL	(*To Molly*) We'd love you to come along as DAVID well, Molly.
MOLLY	(*Looking worried*) So you're saying, both you and Paul want to take me out for a meal tonight?
DAVID	That's right. What do you say?
MOLLY	(*In a state of panic*) Two at once, I couldn't manage that. I'm sorry, I can't make it. (*Searching for an excuse*) I've got to babysit for Claire.
LYN	Molly, you can't turn down an opportunity like this. It'll be a night to remember.
MOLLY	(*Poignantly*) You can say that again.
LYN	Give Claire a ring. She'll soon find someone else. (*Pause*) Can't your husband do it?

MOLLY	(*Unconvincingly*) No, he's out for the night.
DAVID	I've got a friend who may be able to help. I'll give her a ring. (*David dials number on his mobile phone and gets into silent conversation*)
LYN	I'll go and make that cup of tea and then we can sort out the details. (*Exits to kitchen*)
PAUL	(*Taking Molly to side of room away from David*) A little bird's told me that you and the vicar were having a bit of fun the other day.
MOLLY	(*Trying to look innocent*) I don't know what you mean.
PAUL	Molly, you don't need to justify your actions to me. All I'm saying is, be careful. We don't know much about the vicar yet. There's talk that he's getting a bit of a reputation where women are concerned.
MOLLY	What are you implying?
PAUL	We may have a randy reverend in the rectory. (*Pause*) I'll go and help Lyn with the tea. (*Paul exits to kitchen. David switches off his mobile phone*)
DAVID	I'm afraid she can't help. She's going out. (*Pause*) Molly, I can't get you out of my mind. (*Getting close to Molly*) You've scrambled my brains. I lay awake all night just thinking about you. You've awoken feelings I never realized existed. When you kissed me the other day it was like turning a light switch on.
MOLLY	I didn't mean to shock you …
DAVID	As I sat on your bed sensual thoughts were flooding through my mind. Let's just say I needed to do some serious praying that night.
MOLLY	(*Moving away*) I just panicked. My bedroom seemed the only option.
DAVID	You've got a lovely chest.
MOLLY	(*Looking shocked*) I beg your pardon?

DAVID	In your bedroom. I spotted it when I was up there. It must be a useful storage space. Where did you buy it?
MOLLY	(*Looking relieved*) Oh, that. It came from the local furniture store.
DAVID	So what are we going to do?
MOLLY	What about? My chest?
DAVID	No, what are we going to do about you and me?
MOLLY	Take a seat for a minute. You deserve an explanation. (*David sits on a chair*) When my husband walked out, I was devastated.
DAVID	I'm sure you were.
MOLLY	I knew I had to do something to turn my life around. I'd got this person hanging around my neck who'd caused me untold grief.
DAVID	(*Looking mystified*) Hanging around your neck?
MOLLY	I wear a locket with a picture of James and me on our wedding day. (*Walking over to David and opening locket to show him*) I've been going to throw it away, but I can't bring myself to do it. (*David looks into locket, getting close to Molly. Paul, who is holding his mobile phone, enters from kitchen with Lyn*)
PAUL	It's all off. (*David tries to stand up but pulls Molly down so she finishes up sitting on his lap*)
LYN	Are you all right, David?
DAVID	I'm fine, thank you. Molly was just showing me her locket.
LYN	(*Sarcastically*) Really? (*David and Molly stand up*)
PAUL	I've just had a call from my son. The builders won't be finished in time. They've postponed the restaurant opening till next week.

MOLLY	(*Looking upward*) Thank you, God. I mean, we can get things sorted out by then. (*Doorbell rings – Molly exits to hall – Off*) What are you doing here? (*Steve enters, carrying fish and chips – followed by Molly*)
STEVE	(*To Molly*) I've brought fish and chips for the two of us. I'm treating you to a meal. (*Looking at Paul, David and Lyn*) Hello everyone.
DAVID	(*Shaking Steve's hand*) Nice to meet you again. (*Looking at his greasy hand and wiping it on a cushion*)
STEVE	I'm not interrupting anything, am I?
PAUL	Not at all.
STEVE	(*To Molly*) We'll need a couple of plates.
MOLLY	(*Looking bemused*) They're in the cupboard, by the cooker.
STEVE	Won't be a sec. (*Exits to kitchen*)
LYN	What an extraordinary plumber. All the ones I've ever dealt with have only been interested in ripping me off.
PAUL	I must say, I've never had any tradesmen treating me to a meal.
MOLLY	(*Searching for excuse*) He's just started his own business and he's trying to offer a friendly service.
DAVID	What a refreshing attitude.
MOLLY	(*Unconvincingly*) He's sorting out my central heating.
STEVE	(*Entering from kitchen carrying two plates and tomato sauce*) I've found some plates and the tomato sauce.
LYN	Actually, I've been going to ask Molly for your phone number. My mother's got a few problems. Do you service old boilers?
STEVE	(*Looking vague*) I'm happy to give anyone a going over irrespective of age.

PAUL	(*To Steve*) I dabbled in a bit of plumbing many years ago.
MOLLY	(*Trying to change subject*) Yes, well, I'm sure Steve doesn't want to keep talking about work.
PAUL	(*Ignoring Molly*) Do you still use nipple connectors in your job?
STEVE	(*Totally bewildered*) You what?
PAUL	How about when you're working on joints? Do you still rub in flux?
STEVE	Flux? That's a new one on me. I've always used sweet almond oil on the joints. In fact that's what I rub all over their bodies.
MOLLY	I really must insist we give Steve a break.
STEVE	Don't worry about me. Mind you, we don't want the chips getting cold.
PAUL	What do you do if someone's got a problem with leaking gas?
STEVE	(*Unaware Paul is on about plumbing*) Cover them with a towel and discreetly leave the room.
PAUL	Surely you should ring the gas suppliers?
STEVE	(*Looking vague*) Am I missing something here?
LYN	I suggest we leave you to your meal. (*To Molly*) We'll have our tea and chat at a more convenient time. (*Looking at David*) Although it looks as though everything's going to work out. (*Holding David's hand*) Come on, David.
DAVID	Oh, right. (*Sensuously*) See you soon, Molly. Let's hope the plumber gets you going.
MOLLY	(*With trepidation*) I'm sure he will.
STEVE	(*Sitting at the table*) I've put some salt and vinegar on it. I hope that's all right?

PAUL   Enjoy your fish and chips.

DAVID   Bye.

(*Lyn, Paul and David exit to hall. Molly stands looking at Steve who is already eating the fish and chips*)

STEVE   I suggest you get stuck in before it gets cold. (*Molly sits at table and starts eating the fish and chips*)

Blackout

Scene III

When the curtain rises the stage is empty. The doorbell rings. After a few seconds it rings again. Molly enters from kitchen wearing a dressing gown and slippers. She looks radiant, whilst appearing to be exhausted. She exits to hall.

MOLLY   (*Off*) Hello, Fiona. Come in.

FIONA   (*Entering from hall, followed by Molly*) I've been trying to phone you for the past two hours.

MOLLY   I decided to have a bit of a lie-in.

FIONA   You're not kidding. It's nearly lunchtime. When there wasn't any reply, I thought something must be wrong.

MOLLY   (*Looking ecstatic*) Nothing's wrong. In fact, everything's wonderful.

FIONA   (*Looking at Molly*) Hang on a minute. You look blissfully exhausted, and considering you've just got up that can only mean one thing. (*Pause*) So, tell me all about it? Don't spare any details.

MOLLY   Have you ever wondered what heaven's like? For two hours last night and an hour this morning, I've been given an exclusive preview.

FIONA   So, after all these years of marriage, your husband's still able to deliver the goods.

MOLLY	Who said anything about my husband? I'm talking about Mister Adonis from the Sunrise Health Spa.
FIONA	(*Looking shocked*) You didn't, did you?
MOLLY	(*Looking pleased with herself*) I'm afraid I did.
FIONA	So you're saying he called round out of the blue? Whisked you off to an exclusive restaurant, where he wined and dined you? (*Looking thoughtful*) Let me guess. I bet you had goat's cheese and pear salad, followed by lobster, washed down with a bottle of Dom Perignon? I suppose then it was off to a lavish five star hotel, where he made love to you on a four-poster bed, covered with silk sheets?
MOLLY	Not exactly. We sat at that table, had fish and chips washed down with a bottle of beer. Then for dessert we went upstairs where he brought a whole new meaning to the banana split.
FIONA	I've heard of sex on the cheap, but this is taking the mickey.
MOLLY	There was nothing cheap about last night. He not only made the earth move, he shook the complete universe. (*Reflectively*) In all my twenty-one years of marriage, I've never been brought to the boil before. Then last night it happened. (*Pause*) Several times. Over the past few hours I've been combining sexual gymnastics with the 'Kama Sutra'.
FIONA	So where's the incredible hulk now?
MOLLY	I've no idea. He left me in bed, semi-comatose.
FIONA	So what happens now?
MOLLY	You tell me. I've got the choice of a virgin vicar, an inept spouse, or a lusty lover.
FIONA	It doesn't get much better than that.

MOLLY	A month ago I was facing the world on my own. I've now got three men vying for my attention. One's offering me heaven on earth, one's offering me the prospect of going to heaven and the other one's offering me heaven knows what? You're my best friend, what shall I do?
FIONA	(*Getting book from her handbag and reading it*) There's only one thing you can do. You've got to complete the final challenge. You've turned your life around from being a spectator to a partaker, and that's all down to the Marital merry-go-round.
MOLLY	Actually, you're right, I'm going for it. I'll let fate decide my future. So what have I got to do?
FIONA	For the next twenty-four hours, you've got to say yes to everything. The author states that by now you should be able to deal with anything life throws at you, and to prove this to yourself, you must accept whatever's on offer.
MOLLY	So you're saying the answer's yes, whatever the question?
FIONA	You've got it. (*Putting book into her handbag*) Do you realize once you've completed this final task, you've successfully got through every challenge. Actually, I'm very proud of you.
MOLLY	(*Looking pleased with herself*) There've certainly been times when I felt like giving up.
FIONA	Here's a little gift from me as a memento of your achievements. (*Handing over a rabbit's foot*)
MOLLY	Oh, thank you. It's wonderful. (*Looking at rabbit's foot*) What is it?
FIONA	A rabbit's foot good luck charm. My auntie gave it to me. She took it everywhere. Well, that was until she got run over by a lorry. (*Pause*) So how do you feel about what you've achieved?
MOLLY	It's been like a miracle cure. It's made me realize that I can do anything with my life. I'm not beholden to anyone anymore.

FIONA	That's exactly what the author says. At the end of the book she states, "By now you'll be a whole woman again." (*Doorbell rings. Molly exits to hall*)
MOLLY	(*Off*) Hello, Nancy, Paul. Come in.
	(*Molly enters, followed by Nancy and Paul, who are both wearing cycle outfits*)
NANCY	Hello, Fiona. (*Looking at Molly*) I hope we've not called at an inconvenient time.
MOLLY	Not at all. I didn't get much sleep last night. I've had a lot on my mind lately.
NANCY	We've got a bit of good news. (*Looking at Paul*) You tell them, dear.
PAUL	Nancy and I are getting together. We've decided that seeing as we're both on our own, we're going to be companions for each other. She's become my little angel.
FIONA	(*Sarcastically*) Don't you mean Hell's Angel? (*Searching for excuse*) Um … Riding around on your bikes in your leathers.
NANCY	That reminds me. (*To Paul*) My bike's making a terrible noise, it's like a squawking crow. It keeps going (*making the sound of a squawking crow*) ahrr … ahrr …
PAUL	That'll be the gears.
NANCY	Can you do it?
PAUL	I'm sure I can. (*Making the sound of a squawking crow*) Ahrr … ahrr …
NANCY	No dear, I mean, can you fix my gears?
PAUL	Oh, right. Yes, I'll soon sort them out.
NANCY	(*Sensuously*) Thank you, you're wonderful.

PAUL	Tell them what we're planning to do then dear.
NANCY	We're having an open evening at my house, to let people know what's happening.
PAUL	I've been taking my camera on the biking trips and captured some amazing wildlife shots. So as part of our evening's get together, we'll be looking through them.
FIONA	(*Unconvincingly*) That's great. It should be a lot of fun.
NANCY	I'm glad you said that, because we'd like you both to come along.
FIONA	I'm sorry, but I'm out that night.
NANCY	(*Looking surprised*) We've not told you what night it is yet.
FIONA	Haven't you? Oh, so what night is it?
PAUL	A week Tuesday.
FIONA	(*Searching for an excuse*) I've already promised an old school friend I'd visit her.
NANCY	What a shame you can't make it. How about you, Molly?
MOLLY	Well, um, actually … (*Looking at Fiona*)
FIONA	You'd love to go, wouldn't you, Molly? She says yes to everything nowadays.
PAUL	We've got at least a couple of hours of photos to get through.
MOLLY	(*Unconvincingly*) I can't wait to see them.
NANCY	I suggest we make an early start. Let's say about seven-thirty.
MOLLY	(*Reluctantly*) I'll put it in my diary now. (*Writing in diary*)

NANCY	We must go. We're on our way to invite Lyn. (*Walking to hall exit*) Talking of which, did you hear what happened the night she put that rugby player up? (*Discreetly*) According to Paul's nephew, it appears they indulged in a night of passion.
FIONA	(*Looking at Molly*) Strikes me everyone's at it nowadays.
PAUL	(*Looking disappointed*) Not everyone.
CLAIRE	(*Entering from hall*) Hi.
NANCY	I'm glad you're here, Claire. What are you doing a week Tuesday? (*Unseen by Paul or Nancy, Fiona frantically signals to Claire to say she's busy*)
CLAIRE	Um … well … (*Seeing Fiona's signals*) We're taking Tom to a friend's birthday party.
NANCY	What a pity. We're having a get together.
PAUL	We must go, or we'll never deliver all the invitations.
NANCY	See you soon. Bye. (*Nancy and Paul exit to hall*)
FIONA	(*To Claire*) You owe me big time. I've just saved you from an extremely boring evening. (Pause) By the way, have you heard about Lyn's night of passion? She's finally lost her innocence.
MOLLY	We shouldn't be spreading gossip like that.
CLAIRE	Don't worry about me. (*Unconvincingly*) My lips are sealed. (*Pause*) I've got a big favour to ask you, Mum. Could you have Tom for a couple of days next month? (*Getting excited*) My husband's treating me to a short break in Paris. (*Awkwardly*) We're going on the tenth and coming back on the twenty-first.
MOLLY	(*Writing in diary*) Hang on a minute, that's not a couple of days, it's almost a couple of weeks.
CLAIRE	(*Trying to look innocent*) Is it? Oh, yeah. I suppose it is. (*Kissing Molly*) Thank you so much, Mum.

MOLLY	(*Looking fed up*) Think nothing of it.
CLAIRE	I've got to pop to the shops for some paracetamol.
MOLLY	What is it, a migraine headache?
CLAIRE	No, it's a husband headache.
FIONA	I'll come with you. I need to replenish my wine stock. Goodness knows where it all goes. (*Hugging Molly*) Keep me posted. (*Aside – to Molly*) You've come this far. Stick with it, and you'll be another success story in the Marital merry-go-round. Bye. (*Fiona and Claire exit to hall*)
CLAIRE	(*Off*) The Vicar's here, I'll send him in.
DAVID	(*Off*) Hello.
MOLLY	(*Shouting to hall*) Come in, David. (*David enters from hall*) Please excuse me; I'm having a bit of a lazy day.
DAVID	I'm sorry to bother you, Molly, but I need to know where I stand.
MOLLY	(*Sitting on sofa*) In that case, you'd better sit down. (David sits on sofa with Molly) There are a few things we need to sort out. When I kissed you the other day …
DAVID	It was wonderful.
MOLLY	Please, let me finish. I did it, well, let's just say it was something I had to do.
DAVID	(*Looking confused*) I don't understand.
MOLLY	Please don't ask me to explain why. I can assure you I had a very good reason. But having said that, I don't want you getting the wrong idea about the two of us.
DAVID	But you gave me that note, saying you wanted to move our friendship on.
MOLLY	That note wasn't from me, it was from Lyn. She's the one who's always wanted to be with you.

DAVID   Not anymore. I told her the truth about you kissing me. She said she doesn't want anything more to do with me. She got very cross saying I'd betrayed her trust.

MOLLY   If circumstances were different, I'd snap you up like a shot. But as things are, that's not to be.

DAVID   (*With great sorrow*) I guess I'm never going to find myself a partner.

MOLLY   Of course you will. You've got a lot to offer.

DAVID   Do you really think so?

MOLLY   Yes, I do. Don't waste any more time. Today's the important one. (*Pause*) Do you fancy a cup of tea?

DAVID   Well, yes, that would be nice.

MOLLY   I'll put the kettle on.

DAVID   May I pop up to your bedroom? (*Pause*) I'd like to have another look at your chest. I'm seriously thinking of buying one.

MOLLY   Help yourself. (*David exits to hall. Molly walks to kitchen exit. Doorbell rings. Molly exits to hall – Off*) Hello, Lyn. I need to have a word with you. Come in. (*Molly and Lyn enter from hall*) David's upstairs in my bedroom.

LYN   (*Wearing a low cut neckline dress*) Now why doesn't that surprise me?

MOLLY   (*Getting cross*) For your information, he's thinking of buying a bedroom cabinet and wants to get one similar to mine.

LYN   From what you're wearing, it looks as though you two have been at it again. (*Getting cross*) There wasn't any bee the other day. The only reason David was in a state of undress is because you'd defrocked him.

MOLLY   You don't know what you're talking about.

LYN   It's fairly obvious to me, that having lost your own husband, you're after any bit of spare that comes your way.

MOLLY	(*Getting cross*) Nothing could be further from the truth. And while we're on the subject of grabbing a bit of spare, Little Miss High and Mighty, I have it on very good authority that you had an interesting night with a certain rugby player.
LYN	(*Trying to look innocent*) I haven't got a clue what you're on about.
MOLLY	(*Getting cross*) All your sanctimonious talk about saving yourself until your honeymoon. The truth is you're no different than any other woman. At the sight of a young virile man, it's lights out, knickers down.
LYN	(*Getting cross*) How dare you!
MOLLY	What happened with David the other day was none of his making. The simple fact is he was an innocent victim who happened to be in the wrong place at the right time.
LYN	You still haven't told me what went on.
MOLLY	And I probably never will. Just take my word for it. David's a wonderful man. If you let him slip away, you'll regret it for the rest of your life.
LYN	So, are you going to tell him about my little indiscretion?
MOLLY	Of course I'm not. What sort of person do you think I am?
DAVID	(*Entering from hall*) Oh, hello, Lyn. I've just been upstairs, checking out Molly's chest, I mean, cabinet.
MOLLY	I'll make us all a cup of tea. It might help to calm everyone down. (*Exits to kitchen*)
DAVID	(*With trepidation*) So, how have you been since our little chat?
LYN	(*Getting cross*) How could you do that to me, David? How could you throw yourself at Molly, like that?
DAVID	(*Defensively*) I can assure you I didn't throw myself at her. On the contrary, she launched herself at me.

LYN	So where do I stand in all this?
DAVID	I didn't realize until just now that the note was from you.
LYN	I fell in love with you on the day we met. It was pouring with rain. You were soaked to the skin. I knew from that moment I wanted to spend my life with you.
DAVID	What a pity. (*Getting flustered*) I mean, what a pity that I was unaware of your feelings.
LYN	Why do you think I'm always calling round with cakes and pastries?
DAVID	I assumed you enjoyed baking.
LYN	I can't stand baking.
DAVID	I guess when you helped me paint the kitchen, it wasn't because you liked decorating?
LYN	I hate it. (*Seductively*) I just wanted to be with you.
DAVID	I've been a total idiot. (*Looking into Lyn's eyes*) What can I say? (*Staring at Lyn's cleavage*) Apart from the fact that I love your new outfit.
LYN	I'm surprised you've even noticed.
DAVID	(*Unconvincingly*) I can't think what drew my attention to it.
LYN	So where do we go from here?
DAVID	To a restaurant. (*Pause*) May I buy you lunch? It's what you suggested in your note. That'll give us a chance to talk about our future.
LYN	(*Looking surprised*) Oh, right. That would be lovely.
MOLLY	(*Entering from kitchen with cups of tea*) Tea up.
LYN	I'm sorry, Molly, but could we leave the tea for now? David's offered to take me out to lunch.

MOLLY   (*Looking pleased*) That's fine by me. Enjoy yourselves.

LYN   (*Aside to Molly*) Please forgive me for losing my cool. I'm sure we're both going to be discrete about what's happened. (*Pause*) Bye.

DAVID   Bye. (*Lyn and David exit to hall*)

MOLLY   One down, two to go. (*Dials number on phone*) Hello, James, it's me … Where are you? … That's great, I'd like you to pop round here, now… All right, see you in a minute? … Bye. (*Replaces receiver and exits to kitchen. Doorbell rings. Molly enters from kitchen and exits to hall – Off*) Hello, Steve. You'd better come in.

STEVE   (*Entering from hall with Molly*) How are you?

MOLLY   Apart from the fact I've not had the energy to get dressed, I'm absolutely wonderful thanks to you.

STEVE   I've only got a couple of minutes. They need me back at the health spa, but before I go, there's something I need to ask you. What I said the other day about liking the more mature woman.

MOLLY   Let me guess. (*Looking sceptical*) You didn't really mean it.

STEVE   On the contrary. After last night, I realized I want to get to know you much better.

MOLLY   Are you serious?

STEVE   I've never been more serious about anything in my whole life. (Getting close to Molly) I've got my own accommodation at the health spa. I want you to move in with me. I realize we know very little about each other, but sometimes in life you've just got to let fate take its course. So what do you say?

MOLLY   (*Looking thoughtful*) What can I say? I'm supposed to complete all of the challenges. It's got to be yes!

STEVE   Great. (*Kissing Molly*) I'll get things organised. Give me a ring on my mobile if you need me.

MOLLY	I can't remember where I've put your number.
STEVE	(*Taking out his mobile and looking at number*) Let me give it to you again.
MOLLY	Hang on a minute. (*Getting pen and paper*) Right. (*Jotting down number as Steve reads it out*)
STEVE	(*Looking at phone*) 07815683586 (*Steve kisses Molly. He inadvertently leaves his mobile phone on the sideboard*) I'll be in touch a bit later today. Bye. (*Exits to hall*)
MOLLY	(*Sitting on a chair, talking aloud*) What have I done? (*Turns radio on – it is playing 'Everybody's got to learn some time' by The Korgis*)
JAMES	(*Off*) Hello, can I come in? (*Entering from kitchen*) Been having a bit of a lie-in?
MOLLY	Yes. I was up most of last night. (*Pause*) We need to have a serious talk. (*Turns radio volume down low*)
JAMES	(*Sitting on sofa*) I don't like the sound of this.
MOLLY	Over the last few days, my life's been a rollercoaster. I just want to get back to some form of normality.
JAMES	And we will, I promise you. (*Telephone rings. Molly answers it*)
MOLLY	Hello … Oh, hello, Kay … Oh right, I see … So your car won't start? I'll tell you what, James is here. I'll send him over … All right … Bye. (*Replaces receiver*) Would you pop over the road? Kay's got a dentist appointment and can't start her car.
JAMES	Oh, all right. I'll see what I can do. I won't be a minute. (*Exits to kitchen. Steve's mobile phone rings*)
MOLLY	Oh, Steve's left his mobile. (*Answering mobile*) Hello … No, Steve's not here … Yes, I'll give him a message … Really? Okay. I'll tell him. Bye. (*Switches off mobile*)

STEVE	(*Off*) I think I've left my mobile here. (*Steve enters from hall*)
MOLLY	You've just had a call from your girlfriend.
STEVE	Which one? I mean, what was her name?
MOLLY	Felicia, I said you'd ring her. (*Pause*) This is never going to work, Marital merry-go-round or not. (*Handing Steve his mobile*)
STEVE	What are you going on about, Molly?
MOLLY	I've got so close to completing all my challenges.
STEVE	Are you feeling all right?
MOLLY	I've never felt better in my whole life. (*Looking thoughtful*) Sometimes you've got to go with your instincts. (*With sincerity*) I can't do this. I'm very flattered that you want to be with me, and last night was unbelievable. But I know we'd both live to regret it.
STEVE	I don't understand. Look, you and I are great together. From the first time we met it was as though we'd known each other for years. All right, there is a slight age gap, but so what?
MOLLY	(*Holding Steve's hand*) I'll cherish those fleeting precious moments we spent together till my grave. You've actually made me feel like a real woman. I owe you so much, but I love my husband, faults and all. I'm so sorry, but try and understand. (*Letting go of Steve's hand*)
JAMES	(*Off*) Can I come in?
MOLLY	Yes, we're in here.
JAMES	(*Entering from kitchen*) Hi.
MOLLY	Steve was just leaving. He's sorted out all my problems.
JAMES	(*Shaking Steve's hand*) Thank you for all you've done for, Molly. You've helped her through a difficult time. I've never been much of a handyman myself.

STEVE	(*To James*) I can assure you the pleasure was all mine. (*To Molly*) Are you sure about this?
MOLLY	I'm absolutely certain.
STEVE	(*With sorrow*) In that case, I'll leave you to it. Bye. (*Exits to hall*)
JAMES	What a nice lad. I hope you've kept his phone number.
MOLLY	(*Looking surprised*) Whatever for?
JAMES	In case we have any more plumbing problems.
MOLLY	Actually, I'm hoping we can manage without his help.
JAMES	I suppose we could always use old Bert. You know, that plumber who retired ten years ago, lives just up the road.
MOLLY	I don't think he'd have the energy, at his age. (*Pause*) I'm ready to give our marriage another go.
JAMES	(*Hugging Molly*) That's wonderful. I've missed you so much.
MOLLY	We must never take each other for granted again.
JAMES	That'll never happen. I've missed cuddling up to you in bed. I bet you've missed making love.
MOLLY	(*Looking guilty*) I certainly have.
JAMES	Don't worry, now I'm here, everything'll be back to normal.
MOLLY	(*Unconvincingly*) Great. (*Philosophically*) It's my birthday next week, another year gone.
JAMES	I haven't forgotten. What would you like for a present?
MOLLY	There's a health spa that's very nice. It's about fifty miles away. Would you buy me a voucher so if I ever start feeling low, I can treat myself to a massage?
JAMES	Of course I will, my darling. What's it called?

MOLLY   (*With affection*)   'Sunrise Health Spa.'

JAMES   I'll tell you what. (*Walking to the phone*) I'll give them a
              ring now and book you in for a massage next week.
              (*Looking thoughtful*) In fact I'll do better than that.
              (*Pause*) I'll come with you.

(*Molly looks aghast*)

Blackout

BY THE SAME AUTHOR

LOVE BEGINS AT FIFTY (Modern Farce)
M3 F6
This fast and furious farce was first published in 1998 and has never looked back as production follows production. Described by one critic as being up to the highest standard of Ray Cooney - praise indeed.

IT MUST BE LOVE (Farcical Comedy)
M3 F6
Another hilarious play by Raymond Hopkins, with a wedding as the main topic. Enjoyed a highly successful summer season at Torquay.

LOVE AND MONEY (Farcical Comedy)
M4 F4
Another farce from one of the masters of the art. "Never a dull moment – easily staged in one set"   AMATEUR STAGE

LOVE AND PERFECT HARMONY (A Comedy with Music)
M4 F5
This is the fifth play by Raymond Hopkins. Here we have the trials and tribulations of the local choral society. Can be performed with a minimum of scenery.

THE LOVE NEST (Farcical Comedy**)**
M3 F7
David and Janet Thompson were deeply in love when they married thirty-two years ago. That was until Janet's mother moved in with them. In a last attempt to save the marriage, the couple return to the guest house where they spent their honeymoon. But this is doomed from the beginning. The mother-in-law decides to come with them and upsets everybody. David is pursued by an overzealous waitress, a frustrated newly-wed and an admirer from the past. Will true love win through in the end? Only Tyson, the mouse, has the answer.

OTHER PLAYS PUBLISHED BY
SILVERMOON PUBLISHING
www.silvermoonpublishing.co.uk

Nativity
by Jonathan Hall
(2m, 3f)
It's December 1979 and class 2G are getting ready for the school Nativity. Gemma wants to be Mary but because she's got a big loud voice she's the narrator, and anyway Sarah her best friend is far loads prettier than her, everyone says so. And as for Kirsty- she doesn't even get a look in, not that she cares, she's bothered about showing her knickers in the practical area. And of course there can only be one choice for Joseph, and that'd have to be Tony, everyone's favourite, complete with his thirteen colour biro. And Nicholas? In love with Sarah and dreams of flying through the milky way with her in the TARDIS? He's always going to be the Innkeeper.

Nativity is about the play we've all been in. About tea towels on heads and coconut-shell donkey hooves. Dinner ladies and toilet roll angels, reading books and Blue Peter. It's about our six year old selves, the adults that shaped us, the dreams that lit our days- and the people we have become.

I Gave You My Heart
by David Muncaster
(2f)
Kate has received a parcel through the post from her ex-boyfriend. Her sister, Jenny thinks it is sweet, sending her a nice little parting gift. But Dan isn't sweet according to Kate. He's a freak a weirdo. And whatever is in that box is somehow related to the last thing that he wrote on Kate's Facebook page – "I gave you my heart"

Flushed
by Ron Nicol
(3f)
It's a singles night, and Jan and Meg are taking a break in the Ladies Room. Jan is criticising Tara, unaware that Tara is hiding in one of the toilet cubicles. When Tara's
presence is revealed a fight ensues and Jan confesses the reason for her jealousy. Then Meg discovers that the door to the room seems to be locked, and the succeeding series of mishaps and misfortunes ruins Jan's appearance and assurance. Tara eventually manages to open the door, but on the threshold of escape they find that Meg is trapped in one of the cubicles.

A Beginner's Guide To Murdering Your Husband
by David Muncaster
(3f,2m)
This play is presented as though it is an instructional video that the audience are watching being filmed. Maddy will present a variety of methods for disposing of an unwanted husband, aided by Jim, her real life husband, and her faithful employees. But is she really trying to get rid of her husband? Is the video just a ruse to lull him into a false sense of security? The parallels with their real life relationship give Jim plenty to worry about but, as the play reaches its its climax, we realise that nothing is what it seems. Criss-cross indeed!

Understanding Women
by Devon Williamson
(3f,1m)
Mike, Dave and Julian spend a weekend in a garden shed determined to break an age-old mystery. Armed with a case of beer, a box of girlie magazines and a holy book they are going to "understand women". What they discover is not quite what they expected. Understanding Women is a comedy play for both sexes!

Crazy Ladies
by Devon Wiliamson
(5f,1m)
Pamela Browne has organized a 25 year reunion for her four best High school friends. From the moment Kay, now a chocoholic gun toting funeral director, arrives the wheels begin falling off Pamela's meticulously planned weekend. Added to the mix is Sandy, who is now a Nun, Dianne, married the school nerd and a mother of eight sons, Rachel, a runaway teenager on a mission to dig up some dirt on her mother, and Shaun, the greasy motel janitor. This outrageous comedy is a rollercoaster ride of emotion.

www.ingramcontent.com/pod-product-compliance
Lightning Source LLC
Chambersburg PA
CBHW060140050426
42448CB00010B/2227